DAVID A. BARTON

D1322960

Discovering
Chapels and
Meeting Houses

SHIRE PUBLICATIONS LTD

Contents

British Library Cataloguing in Publication Data: Barton, David A. Discovering chapels and meeting houses - (Discovering books number 209) - 3rd edition I. England. Nonconformist churches. Building, history. I. Title. 942. ISBN 0-7478-0097-9.

Cover: The Friends' Meeting House at Jordans, Buckinghamshire.

For Gwyneth, Deirdre and Fiona

Copyright © 1975 and 1990 by David A. Barton. First published 1975. Second edition 1990. Number 209 in the 'Discovering' series. ISBN 0 7478 0097 9.

Printed in Great Britain by C. I. Thomas & Sons (Haverfordwest) Ltd, Press Buildings, Merlins Bridge, Haverfordwest, Dyfed SA61 1XF.

1. The nonconformist background

Before we venture to consider the places of worship built by nonconformists, it would be useful to look at the various denominations which through the ages have in their different ways helped to make up the nonconformist tradition.

The beginnings of dissent

While dissent in England may be said to begin with Wycliffe and the Lollards, no chapels were built as early as this and it is sufficient for our purposes to begin much later with Henry VIII and the break with the Pope. Once the country had been cut off from Catholic allegiance, it remained to be seen what form the English church would take. There were many opinions on this but, broadly speaking, they may be divided into two. There were those puritans who hoped to reform the new church from within and there were those separatists who saw as the only solution the setting up of a new church. In 1567 officials of the city of London paid a visit to Plumbers' Hall, where they found about a hundred people holding a secret service. This is the first recorded instance of a separatist congregation in England after the Reformation and is, as Routley says in *English Religious Dissent* (1960), usually taken to be the first emergence in this country of what is now called Congregationalism. The first rounded character to appear in the history of dissent was Robert Browne, who lived from about 1550 to 1633. He spent much of his long life in prison for preaching separatism and spent some time in Holland. In 1593 John Udall, who was accused of writing puritan tracts, was executed at Tyburn for sedition, together with John Penry, Thomas Cartwright and Thomas Greenwood. The passing of the Conventicle Act in 1592, which made secret religious meetings illegal, and the impact made by the executions of these 'Brownists' in 1593 forced the puritan movement to remain underground and drove the first organised communities overseas, mainly to Holland. In 1620 the Pilgrim Fathers set sail for America, led by John Robinson and William Brewster, exiles from England who had formed a church at Leyden in Holland. Most of the puritan refugees went to Holland and there they formed their own churches. In Holland they learned much from Henry Ainsworth (1570-1622) a former Fellow of St John's College, Cambridge, who became minister to the exiles in Amsterdam in 1596. This continental exile of the puritans had a number of results and in particular played a major part in the rise of the Baptist movement.

The fundamental principle of the Baptist faith is adult baptism, which springs from the belief that baptism should only be administered to those of mature enough age to give personal assent to the sacrament and to take for themselves the vows associated with it. The denomination now known as General Baptist, or more simply Baptist, may be traced back to John Smyth (sometimes called Smith) who was a Fellow of Christ's College, Cambridge, and an Anglican clergyman. He became a separatist and in 1603 had gathered together a congregation at Lincoln. He later emigrated to Amsterdam and began to preach and put into practice adult baptism. Smyth died in 1612 but members of his church returned to London and established a church at Pinners Hall, one of their number, Thomas Helwys (or Helwisse), who died in 1616, being the first minister. Though severely persecuted, as were all dissenters at this period, their numbers steadily increased.

Throughout the reigns of James I and Charles I the puritan movement was forced to remain underground but it still continued to flourish. The number of 'conventicles' (illegal religious meetings) in the London area was eleven in 1631, according to Briggs's *Puritan Architecture and Beyond* (1946), but by 1640 it was estimated to be eighty. In addition to these 'revolutionary' puritans, there were many puritans of a milder kind who were seeking to reform the Anglican church from the inside. As will be readily understood, the circumstances of the time did not permit the building of places of worship, nor even of public services. Congregations at this period were accustomed to meet in private houses, often with sentries posted outside to warn of the approach of trouble. It is therefore surprising to find that some Congregational and Baptist churches may be dated to this period, e.g. the 'Ancient Chapel' of Toxteth near Liverpool (1618, rebuilt 1773), the Baptist chapel at Tewkesbury (dated by Briggs at 1623, but now believed to be a later conversion of a medieval house) and the Congregational chapel at Walpole, Suffolk (1647).

East Anglia and in particular the area around Cambridge was at this time the stronghold of the puritan movement and many puritan preachers occupied livings there. Both Emmanuel College, which was founded in 1584, and Sidney Sussex College, founded in 1596 and Oliver Cromwell's old college, were founded for the purpose of training protestant preachers.

The Presbyterians

By the time of the Civil War, which broke out in 1642, the puritans were beginning to crystallise into two distinct factions, the Presbyterians and the Independents. The Presbyterians, who may be called the moderate puritans, did not strictly become nonconformists until after 1660. Before 1660 the Presbyterians had attempted to reform the Anglican church from within and one of the results of the Westminster Assembly of Divines, which began to meet in 1644, was the formulation of a presbyterian system of church government. This involved the abolition of bishoprics; each parish was governed by the presbytery (i.e. the minister and the elders); delegates from each presbytery were to attend a classical assembly (or classis) which covered a particular area (in Derbyshire, for example, there was a classis for every hundred in the county). Delegates from the classis were to attend a provincial synod and finally delegates from the provincial synods were to attend a general assembly. As far as can be told, the general assembly never met, but there is evidence from various counties to show that the system was working at least as far as the classis. However, their failure to complete the setting up of their system of church government and the restoration of the Anglican hierarchy saw an end to the hopes of the Presbyterians of seeing Presbyterianism prevail and, of the two thousand clergy ejected from their livings in 1662, all except about four hundred were Presbyterians. For many years Presbyterians hoped in vain for a relaxing of the conditions, which would have made it possible for them to re-enter the national church. Their reluctance to set up an independent church stemmed from this hope and partly explains the reason why no Presbyterian church was created. After the Toleration Act of 1689 an attempt, which was not very successful, was made to unite Presbyterians and Independents, and the Presbyterian Fund was set up to help dissenting congregations all over the country. The union between Presbyterians and Independents broke down a few years later as far as London was concerned but union still continued in some other parts of the country. Meanwhile, the Presbyterians were beginning to be affected by Unitarianism which steadily gained ground in spite of the fact that the Toleration Act of 1689 expressly excluded Unitarians from benefit. Many of the meeting houses dating from this period which are now Unitarian were originally Presbyterian.

Most Presbyterian congregations either became Independent or Unitarian. Finally, however, in the nineteenth century, there was a slight revival when the Presbyterian Church in England was founded in 1836-42 in connexion with the Church of Scotland. In 1876 the Presbyterian Church in England and the English section of the United Presbyterian Church of Scotland, of which branches had been in existence in England since 1744, joined together to form the Presbyterian Church of England. Recently, the wheel has turned full circle and the Presbyterian Church in England and the Congregational Church in England have come together to form the United Reformed Church.

The Independents

The history of the Independents, who later became known as Congregationalists is less complex. In the seventeenth century they were in most ways similar to the Baptists. Their main tenet was opposition to all forms of church government and they believed strongly that each individual congregation should have the power to manage its own affairs and choose its own ministers. A small minority of congregations became Unitarian in the eighteenth century and as we have seen some Presbyterian congregations in their turn became Independent. In close association with the Congregationalists was the Connexion founded by Selina, Countess of Huntingdon, about 1780. In the nineteenth century, the Congregationalists formed regional associations and in 1832 the Congregational Union of England and Wales was formed. This Union, with which the Countess of Huntingdon's Connexion maintained a close association, is a voluntary association only and had only moral authority over the churches within it.

The Baptists

Returning now to the Baptists, we find a much more intricate story. There had always been great diversity among English Baptists. The General Baptists in the seventeenth century were Arminian, i.e. they believed in Free Will, as opposed to the Particular Baptists who were Calvinistic and believed in Predestination. During the eighteenth century the General Baptists were strongly influenced by Unitarianism and in 1770 their orthodox section under the leadership of Dan Taylor (1738-1816) formed the New Connexion of General Baptists, which broke away completely in 1803, leaving the old assembly virtually Unitarian. In the latter years of the eighteenth century there were splits in the Particular Baptists when Andrew Fuller (1754-1815) led an evangelical revival and joined with the New Connexion of General Baptists. In 1813 a Particular Baptist, Joseph Ivimey (1773-1834), founded the 'General Union of Baptist Ministers and Churches' which in 1831 was revived to include ministers and churches of the New Connexion of General Baptists. This was a voluntary union of the loosest kind but led ultimately to the foundation of the Baptist Union in 1891,

6

which joined the Particular Baptists and the New Connexion of General Baptists. Many Baptist churches remained outside the Union, particularly in Yorkshire, Norfolk and Suffolk. The Gadsbyites in Yorkshire and Lancashire, led by William Gadsby (1773-1834), were the ultra-conservative wing of the Particular Baptists and had opposed the Fullerites. In East Anglia George Wright (1789-1873) led a similar movement and the Norfolk and Suffolk New Association founded in 1829 still remains outside the Baptist Union. These die-hards became known as the Strict and Particular Baptists. Again in 1861 a schism split even this small group further. The controversy was waged in two rival periodicals, *The Earthen Vessel* (later *The Gospel Herald*) and *The Gospel Standard*. Today, 'The Gospel Standards' have approximately three hundred churches, none of which are in any association. Other Strict and Particular Baptist churches are organised in local associations mainly in East Anglia and London, with a small association in Yorkshire.

The Quakers

The Quakers or, to use their official name, the Society of Friends, have unlike other churches existed, at least in Britain, since the seventeenth century, with only one very small schism. The society was founded by George Fox (1624-91) and having no formal creed has been less prone to controversy. Possibly the most extreme form of the 'Old Dissent', Friends have through the ages been in the forefront of all manner of social reform, being active in penal reform, factory welfare and many forms of philanthropy. Frank and forthright in the expression of. their opinions and contemptuous of empty social customs and formulae, their views, particularly on pacifism and anti-militarism, have at times led them to be extremely unpopular. Their services are distinguished by lack of formality and ritual, they admitted of no paid clergy and their meeting houses are plain and spartan.

The Unitarians

The Unitarians, whom we have met before, tended to form an intellectual aristocracy among Dissenters. As their name suggests, they did not believe in the Trinity but only the Unity of Christ. Christ was to them just an exalted human teacher. While Unitarian views were their main tenet, they disliked both credal tests and ecclesiastical discipline.

The Methodists

With the eighteenth century came the rise of the most prolific chapel-builders of all, the Methodists. John Wesley

(1703-91) was an Anglican clergyman who never formally broke with the Church and who all his life avoided competing with it. The Methodist Society came into being because of opposition to Wesley's evangelism. Wesley and his brother Charles began their field preaching in 1739 and wherever they travelled little groups of converts were left behind who set up Methodist societies. The early Methodists did not have purpose-built chapels but met anywhere a room could be found.

The organisation laid down by Wesley for the early Methodist societies has to a great extent survived and is followed by the Methodist church today, notably the principle of itinerancy by which the ministers move on to a new post at intervals to prevent them from becoming stale and complacent. However, in the fifty or so years after the death of Wesley in 1791, a number of secessions took place and it is as a result of this that so many Methodist chapels were built over the country. The secessions were caused almost always by quarrels over church government and discipline; there was never any question of disagreement on doctrines. The first split came in 1797 when a group led by Alexander Kilham (1762-98) left to form the Methodist New Connexion, popularly known as the Kilhamites. Then in the Staffordshire Potteries in 1811 the Primitive Methodists were founded by Hugh Bourne (1772-1852) and William Clowes (1780-1851). Bourne, influenced by American evangelistic ideas, organised camp meetings (open-air evangelistic meetings on a large scale) on Mow Cop, Staffordshire. The meetings were disowned by the local Wesleyans who thought they would lead to licence and immorality, and Bourne was expelled in 1810. He joined with Clowes, who had also recently been expelled for unauthorised evangelism, and the Primitive Methodist Connexion was born. In organisation the connexion was more democratic than the parent body and was notable for its employment of women preachers. The movement spread and became strong chiefly in the North, Midlands and East Anglia; in numbers it became the second strongest connexion in Methodism. The Independent Methodist originated in the neighbourhood of Manchester in 1806; it changed its name to the United Churches of Christ in 1833, to the United Free Gospel Churches in 1841 and back to the Independent Methodist Churches in 1898. This church still remains independent of the main Methodist body but its numbers are very small. In 1815 William O'Brien (1778-1868), a local preacher of the Wesleyan Methodist circuit, broke away and formed the Bible Christians. They were strong in Devon and Cornwall but also had some chapels in Kent; they did notable missionary work abroad, particularly in China. In 1828 a dispute over the organ at the Brunswick Chapel in Leeds caused the secession of the Protestant Methodists, who joined with the Wesleyan Association, itself the result of a secession of 1836. In 1857 the Wesleyan Association joined with the Methodist Reform Churches (the result of a secession of 1849) to form the United Methodist Free Churches. The minority of the Methodist Reform Churches who did not join the Wesleyan Association formed the Wesleyan Reform Union in 1859. This church, which still remains independent to this day, is largely active in the Midlands and Yorkshire. In 1907 the Methodist New Connexion, the Bible Christians and the United Methodist Free Churches joined together under the name of the United Methodist Church. In 1932 the United Methodist Church joined with the Primitive Methodist Church and the Wesleyan Methodists, the original body, to form the Methodist Church.

Other denominations

It remains to mention the other churches, mostly of nineteenth-century origin, which have built chapels in the British Isles. The 'citadels' of the Salvation Army have never received the attention they deserve and there are some interesting examples, notably at Aberdeen where there is a turreted citadel and in Oxford Street, London, where the Regent Hall was converted from a skating rink in the 1880s. The Army was founded by William Booth (1829-1912) in 1865 and received its present form and title in 1878. It rejects all sacraments, places much emphasis on the moral side of Christianity and does much useful social work.

The Plymouth Brethren are so named because the first centre in England was established by J. N. Darby (1800-82) at Plymouth in 1832. They are split into two fundamental groups, the Open Brethren and the Exclusive Brethren. Their outlook is puritanical and they have no organised ministry, but great stress is laid on the breaking of bread each Sunday and each church is completely autonomous. Their chapels, like those of so many of the nineteenth-century denominations, canot be classified—Betjeman says that they are like a cross between a Quaker meeting house and a Primitive Methodist chapel.

While it would be possible to catalogue many more dissenting sects, such as the Mormons, the Christadelphians, the Four Square Gospellers or the Seventh Day Adventists, it would not further the purpose of this book. Meeting as they most often do in converted or temporary buildings, they never seem to have acquired any definite style of their own.

An exception may be made, however, for the Catholic and Apostolic Church, a church which, though small, in its time built some elaborate chapels. The church arose as a result of the activities of Edward Irving (1792-1834), a powerful preacher, who in 1822 became minister of the Caledonian Church, Hatton Garden, where his congregation grew. In 1826 he was a speaker at a conference at Albury, Surrey, where the squire Henry Drummond became a keen supporter. In 1831 the gift of tongues appeared in Irving's congregation and Irving and the majority of his congregation were excluded from the London Presbytery. His followers founded a new church at Newman Street but Irving himself denied any intention to separate or any exceptional gifts himself. Members of the new connexion were admitted by 'sealing' or the laying on of hands and did not necessarily withdraw from other churches. The ministers were divided into four orders: the apostles, who alone could lay on hands; the prophets, who expounded and exhorted; evangelists, who declared the truth of the gospel; and pastors, who looked after the flock. Presiding over each congregation was an angel or bishop. The elaborate liturgy used was largely derived from Roman Catholic and Greek Orthodox ritual. Seven churches were founded in London and others elsewhere but numbers declined following a split until by 1909 there were only about five thousand members left in England.

Nonconformity in Scotland

In Scotland nonconformity has evolved in a different way and cannot easily be dealt with in a short account. Briefly, the Church of Scotland has been Presbyterian since 1690 and is national, endowed and free. The greater part of the Scottish people belong to the Presbyterian Church and, while Methodism and some of the nineteenth-century dissenting sects have some small following in Scotland, nonconformity as we know it has never been as strong a force there as in England. In Scotland the kirk rather than the chapel is the dominant force.

Nonconformity in Wales

Wales, on the other hand, has always been associated with chapels and it has some very attractive ones. Here again nonconformism developed differently. The growth of puritanism in Wales was slow but the first dissenting chapel was opened at Llanvaches in Gwent in 1638. In the Civil War Wales remained, in general, Royalist and High Church but after the Restoration, due to the continued appointment of English non-resident churchmen, popular support for the

Church of Wales began to decline. The early Welsh Methodists can claim priority in preaching and evangelistic work over the Methodists in England. The first contact between them was in 1739 but before then Griffith Jones of Llanddowror (1684-1761), Howell Harris of Trefecca (1714-43), Daniel Rowland of Llangeitho (1713-90) and William Williams of Pantycelyn (1717-91) had been preaching for some time. Separation from the established church was not completed until 1811 when the first ministers were ordained. The church was formerly known as the Calvinistic Methodist Church but is now known as the Presbyterian Church of Wales. The Baptists, too, have been active in Wales since John Myles (1621-84) organised the first Baptist church in 1649 at Ilston, West Glamorgan, and Vavasour Powell (1617-70) acted as the leader of a band of travelling evangelists. The most famous Baptist preacher was Christmas Evans (1766-1838). Congregationalism in Wales followed very much the English pattern and the Welsh churches joined the Congregational Union of 1832. Thus from a rather slow start dissenters in Wales came to be in the majority. If the 'nonconformist conscience' still retains any force at all, it is in Wales.

It may seem from the above account that nonconformists in England were narrow-minded, argumentative and rather dull. This is not so and judging from the books and university theses of recent years which treat various branches of dissent from a sociological point of view, it seems that there is an awakening of interest in the subject. This is all to the good since we can now try to get an objective view of a phenomenon which has had far too many uncritical apologists in the past.

2. The penal period

Before 1689, as we have seen from the preceding chapter, the early puritans were liable to legal penalties both for not attending church and also for holding unauthorised religious meetings, so it was not until the Toleration Act was passed in 1689 that chapel building could start in earnest.

It is claimed that the oldest chapel in England is the Congregational chapel at **Horningsham,** near Longleat in Wiltshire, which has '1566' carved on the gable end. Local tradition, which does not appear to be confirmed by any documentary proof, tells that the chapel was built in 1566 by Sir John Thynne for the Scottish Presbyterian masons who were building Longleat. Apart from its large windows, the chapel, which is still in excellent condition, could easily be mistaken for a typical Wiltshire farm cottage and, despite extensive renovation and extension in the late eighteenth or early nineteenth century, it is still of great interest. It is thatched and though the box pews have been removed there is still much old woodwork. Lindley, in his book *Chapels and Meeting Houses* (1969), considers that the seating in the side galleries is original, as are the hat pegs on the rear wall of the men's gallery. (Until well into the nineteenth century men and women usually sat on opposite sides of a chapel and the men's side could always be distinguished by its row of hat pegs.) The pulpit is a tall one and complete with a sounding board or tester—a kind of acoustic canopy of wood which was intended to magnify the sound of the preacher's voice. There are two graveyards, one surrounding the chapel, the other across the road, both grassed down.

Possibly the second oldest dissenting chapel in England and certainly the oldest Baptist chapel is in **Tewkesbury,** Gloucestershire. The Old Baptist Chapel, as it is called to distinguish it from the 1805 Barton Street Baptist chapel, is to be found in Church Street, near the Abbey. It is one of a row of small buildings and could easily be overlooked. It cannot be dated exactly but there is a deed in existence, dated 1623, which conveys property to the local Baptist cause but not necessarily the present chapel. The oldest chapel record-book in existence begins in 1655. With some caution therefore it could be said that the chapel was converted from an existing timber-framed building about the middle of the seventeenth century. Some authorities consider the Tewkesbury Baptist Church to be a continuation of a Lollard community—the Lollards being strong in this part of Gloucestershire. Details of the history of the chapel are contained in *Sketch of the History of the Baptist Church, Tewkesbury* by Thomas Wilkinson (undated) and a recent pamphlet, *350 Years of Tewkesbury Baptist Church* (1973).

The alley in which the chapel is situated goes directly to the side of the river Severn, which would probably have been used for baptism in the early days. Between the chapel and the Severn lies the graveyard; one of the cottages in the row used to be the minister's house and another used to be a stable for the horses of the congregation. As at Horningsham, only the large windows of the chapel show that it is different from the other cottages in the row. The tiny building is rectangular with the door and the pulpit on the long side. The walls are panelled and there are plain wooden benches with backs. There is a simple pulpit with plain panelling and the gallery is panelled. The only lighting is from a candelabrum hung from the ceiling. After the building of the Barton Street chapel in 1805, less use was made of the Old Chapel but services were still held there at intervals. During the war, according to a local Baptist chapel member, many services were held there for the American forces stationed nearby. By the mid 1970s the chapel was sadly in need of restoration and the funds of the local chapel were not adequate to cope with such a big project. The Tewkesbury Civic Trust took the matter in hand and restoration is now complete.

Suffolk possesses the second oldest Congregational chapel. This stands on the edge of the village of **Walpole,** near Halesworth, and while a date of 1647 has been quoted it would be safer to say that it was a sixteenth-century house which was converted to a chapel in the seventeenth century. Like the other early chapels, its external appearance is domestic rather than religious. An interesting feature of the building is its double-ridged roof which produces M-shaped gable ends. The roof is supported internally by a central wooden column, said to have been a ship's mast from Great Yarmouth. As is usual in early chapels, the pulpit is in the middle of the long side of the rectangle facing the door. The pulpit, standing between two large round-headed windows, has a canopy over it suspended from one of the roof beams and below it is a small rostrum with a book rest and wooden rail. The box-pews are arranged on three sides of the building facing the pulpit, each pew has a number and a spring catch. Lighting in the chapel is by a candelabrum, by candlesticks on the edges of the pews and by oil lamps. The gallery occupies the three sides facing the pulpit. The chapel is now little used for worship but is used occasionally for concerts.

An example of a chapel which has been tastefully restored is the chapel at **Bramhope,** near Otley in West Yorkshire. To be strictly accurate Bramhope chapel is not nonconformist, since it was built as a Presbyterian chapel in 1649 at a time when the Church of England was Presbyterian, but it is nevertheless worth describing here. Badly damaged in a gale in 1962, the belfry was shattered, but it has since been carefully restored and its interior is especially worth seeing. (It is open to visitors during the summer season and even when closed a key may be obtained from the manager of the Post House Hotel nearby.) It is a plain oblong building of rough-cast stone with a belfry and one bell. The outstanding feature of the interior is a high, roomy three-decker pulpit with desk below and sounding board above. The box-pews are original and ranged on three sides round the pulpit. There are also some benches. The hexagonal font is dated 1673 and the windows are of the straight-headed mullioned type with individual round-arched lights. The chapel was originally built by Robert Dyneley, the Lord of the Manor of Bramhope, and an article by Bryan Dale in the *Bradford Antiquary,* volume 1, details its history.

Other chapels dating from the 'penal' period are the Friends' Meeting House, **Almeley,** Hereford and Worcester, a black and white half-timbered building, typical of the district but unusual for Friends' meeting houses, and carefully restored in 1956; the Friends' Meeting House at **West Adderbury,** Oxfordshire (1675); and the Friends' Meeting House at **Ifield,** West Sussex (1676). Mention should also be made of the 'Ancient Chapel' of **Toxteth,** Liverpool. Reputedly built in 1616, it was the chapel of Richard Mather, the puritan divine, who later emigrated to New England.

3.   1689 to the end of the eighteenth century

As the end of the seventeenth century approached, a more permissive climate for nonconformist worship came about after the Toleration Act of 1689. During the years 1689-1700, 2,418 buildings were registered as places of worship by dissenters. Many of these chapels were enlarged, altered and otherwise 'improved' in the nineteenth century and have lost much of their original charm. Fortunately, some remain unchanged and from these we may deduce the general characteristics of the early purpose-built chapels.

Most chapels of this period, large or small, are modest and retiring and externally have no ecclesiastical features. They were usually brick-built with hipped roofs, i.e. the roofs were sloped on all sides without gables. Tiles were usually used for the roofs; in East Anglia pantiles were so customary that dissenters were often referred to as 'pantilers'. Doorways of the period, while having the usual classical columns, are seldom extravagantly decorated and are usually soundly built in an unobtrusive way. The windows usually had flat or semi-circular arches over them and were leaded with wooden mullions and transoms. An exception to this is the 'Old Meeting' of 1693 at Norwich, which had sash windows—said to be the first sash windows in Norwich.

Before we consider the interiors of the meeting houses of this period, it may be well to look at the Anglican churches which were built at the time, for these had some influence on the better-class meeting house of the period. The pre-

Reformation churches had been built for Catholic worship and adapted, often with some difficulty, for Protestant worship. The Catholic worshipper was a spectator rather than a direct participant and as long as he could see, all was well, but when services in the vernacular were introduced and when the sermon became more important it was essential that the worshipper should not only be able to see but to hear as well. The churches built by Sir Christopher Wren are often known as auditory churches or 'preaching houses' (by their opponents). In these churches Wren gave special importance to the pulpit, preferring the large three-decker type with sounding boards.

Like the Georgian church, the Georgian meeting house was usually oblong in shape. Not many of these meeting houses exist today; those that do are usually in city side streets or in the older market towns. Their length is usually twice their width, and they usually have a door or more often a pair of doors with windows placed symmetrically on either side and on top. The more elegant meeting houses often had oval windows, as at Bury St Edmunds and Ipswich. The communion table, following the dictates of Calvin, occupied a central position in the meeting house, being usually in the midst of the congregation and in front of the pulpit. At some of the more wealthy Presbyterian meeting houses the congregation sat in their pews and the bread and wine was brought to them; in these places there was usually a small symbolic table on a dais with a rail round it. In early Congregational meeting houses it was usual to have a long table which stretched the width of the chapel from beneath the pulpit to the opposite long side. This pew when not in use was usually occupied by poor male church attenders; this practice was still in force at Yarmouth and Ipswich as late as the early twentieth century.

A different feature may be seen in Friends' meeting houses and early Baptist chapels. Instead of a pulpit, there is a long raised bench facing the congregation, known as a stand in Quaker circles, on which the elders sat. There being no paid ministers, the leadership of the meeting was deputed to the senior members.

The pulpit was the most impressive feature in these meeting houses and was usually of three tiers; the sermon was delivered from the top tier, the middle tier was used for prayers and for the lessons, while the bottom tier was reserved for the precentor, who gave out the metrical psalms and the hymns, line by line. On the pulpit even the most austere congregations usually allowed themselves a little decoration, and carving with biblical themes is sometimes seen.

As we have said, East Anglia was ever a stronghold of dissent and one of its most famous meeting houses is **Norwich** 'Old Meeting', built in 1693 and fortunately in excellent condition. Situated in Colegate in the old part of Norwich, it is brick-built and has a tiled roof, hipped and with classical motifs in stone. The front of the building is embellished with pilasters in brick with Corinthian capitals. Beneath one of the windows is a painted sundial giving the date 1693. Inside, the pulpit is on the long side facing the entrance and the gallery occupies three sides. The woodwork is very fine, especially the gallery front and the stairs.

Dating from this period too, and still in regular use, is the Unitarian chapel in St Saviourgate, **York.** This was built in 1693 and is the oldest dissenting chapel still existing in York. It is built in the form of a Greek cross, i.e. a cross with all arms of equal length and in the middle at the intersections is a tower. The roofing is rather unusual in that of the five roofs needed, three are gabled and the other two, those covering the central crossing and the south side, are hipped. The round-headed windows are apparently a late Georgian insertion of about 1830, according to R. Willis's book, *The Nonconformist Chapels of York* (undated), and there is no means of telling the style of the early windows. The marginal lights to the windows are good examples of the use of flashed ruby glass, the white glass forming the ground, while the ruby glass is cut or etched to the pattern. The small gallery has an organ, presented to the chapel about 1800; it was the first chapel in York to have an organ. The pews and communion rail, like the railings outside, date from about 1860, while the hexagonal pulpit is reputed to be late seventeenth-century and could be original. An attractive feature of this chapel are the wall monuments, some of them by local York masons.

Dating from about the same period is the Unitarian chapel at **Knutsford,** Cheshire, which was built in 1689.

'The chapel has a picturesque and old world look . . . The staircases which led to the galleries were outside, at each end of the building, and the irregular floor and worn stone steps looked grey and stained by time and weather. The grassy hillocks, each with little bright headstone, were shaded by a grand old wych-elm and the casement windows of the chapel were made of heavy leaded diamond-shaped panes, almost covered with ivy.'

This description, written by Mrs Gaskell and taken from her novel *Ruth* (1852) still holds good. Together with her husband and daughters, she is buried in the graveyard of Knutsford chapel. The internal furniture of the chapel was renewed in 1859, but the chapel with its whitewashed walls still retains an old world atmosphere. The gallery runs round three sides of the building, entrances to it being by the external staircases described above, while the entrances to the ground floor are directly under them. Mrs Gaskell immortalised Knutsford and its chapel as 'Cranford' in her book of that name.

Two other chapels in Cheshire, not far from Knutsford, are worthy of attention, the King Edward Street Unitarian chapel at **Macclesfield,** built in 1689, and Dean Row Chapel, **Wilmslow,** built in 1693. These three chapels are so much alike that it has been suggested that they were designed by the same hand. These three chapels are fully described in *Old Cheshire Churches* (new edition 1973) by Raymond Richards.

As a contrast to these plain and rather homely Cheshire meeting houses, let us look at the Friar Street Unitarian Chapel at **Ipswich.** Built in 1700 as a Presbyterian chapel by Joseph Clarke, a carpenter, it was one of the best of its date and excited the admiration of Daniel Defoe, who visited Ipswich in 1722. Rectangular in shape, it has a hipped roof, two storeys and a five-bay front, each of the end bays having a door with pilaster and portico. The heads of the doors are charmingly decorated with cherubs. The interior is even more elegant. There is a pulpit standing on a tulip base (attributed by some to Grinling Gibbons); it has rich carvings and delicately curved stairs with twisted balusters. There is the usual seating arrangement with the pulpit on the long south side and the box-pews facing it on three sides. The gallery runs round three sides and the stairs have balusters which are twisted like the pulpit stairs. The gallery clock has on its top a gilt-winged cherub, holding an open music book with the words 'Glory be to God on high, God whose glory fills the skies'. A two-tiered chandelier hangs from the coffered ceiling.

Another Suffolk chapel which is widely praised is the former Unitarian chapel at **Bury St Edmunds.** Built in 1711-12 of red brick, it is now a Pentecostal church. On a smaller scale than the Ipswich chapel, it has a three-bay front and large round-arched windows. There are galleries on three sides and a pulpit facing the entrance. The doorway has pilasters and a pediment.

At **Winslow** in Buckinghamshire is a small Baptist Chapel, known as Keech's Meeting House, from its association with Benjamin Keech (1640-1704), a celebrated Baptist preacher, who was pastor here from 1660. It may well be one of the oldest chapels in the county and may be tentatively dated to 1695. It stands in a small graveyard with tombstones and the interior is partly paved with memorial stones. There is an old pulpit, with a deacon's chair in front of it, an old pewter communion cup, a narrow gallery and a desk folding flat to the wall on which children were taught to read and write. This chapel is little-known compared with some but the Royal Commission on Historical Monuments thought it worthy of preservation in their report published in 1913.

Chesterfield in Derbyshire has another little-known Unitarian chapel in Elder Yard, not far from the church. This chapel, still in regular use, was completed in 1694 and was first used by Congregationalists and Presbyterians jointly but the Congregationalists withdrew and it later became wholly Unitarian. The original chapel seems to have been a plain rectangular building about 50 feet long by about 25 feet wide with the almost obligatory hipped roof, a gallery and the pulpit on the middle of the long side facing the entrance. During its long history, alterations have been made, notably in 1821; it has been enlarged, a chancel built and the altar moved. D. W. Robson's book *Origins and History of Elder Yard Chapel* (1924) gives the history and catalogues the changes made in the fabric and the interior.

Chinley chapel, also in Derbyshire, was built slightly later, in 1711, in the village of Chinley near Chapel-en-le-Frith. In 1686 and earlier the original Chinley congregation, led by the Rev. William Bagshawe, an ejected minister known as the 'Apostle of the Peak', were meeting in a barn at nearby Malcoff Farm, where the farmer was sympathetic to dissenters. When the farm changed hands the new owner was not as friendly and the congregation moved to Chinley. The area at this time seems to have been very unfavourable to dissent, chapel-goers were often molested on the way to service, and during the building of the chapel a guard was posted every night to prevent damage to the building. Even today on the mullioned windows can be seen stout hooks which supported shutters to protect the windows. The chapel itself is two-storeyed and built of local stone and might easily pass for a house. It is surrounded by a graveyard with imposing tombstones. The minister to the congregation from 1702 to 1755 was the Rev. Dr James Clegg, who was also qualified in medicine. Derbyshire Record Society have published the first complete edition of Clegg's diary, which gives a vivid picture of life in this remote part of Derbyshire.

At about the same time in **Great Warford** in Cheshire a small Baptist chapel was being converted from a barn and a cottage. A congregation of Baptists in the district had been meeting secretly since at least 1668 and by 1712 numbers had grown so much that a larger building was needed. The original building, from which the chapel was converted, is said to date from early Tudor times and the north side of this was left undisturbed in the conversion. This side is still intact and has a framework of beams consisting of ten uprights and four horizontals at different levels and as the original wattle and daub has perished the panels have been bricked in. The roof is apparently original and has projecting eaves. The chapel is very small, only about 20 feet by 15 feet, and the furnishings seem to be original. The panelled pulpit is placed against the west wall; there are pews for sixty-two people and a little gallery at the east end. At right angles to the chapel is the little cottage, where formerly the minister lived, spoiled however by modern renovation. More information about this interesting chapel may be found in G. J. Barber's book *A Peep into Baptist History in Cheshire* (1936).

In the village of **Aston Tirrold,** Oxfordshire, is the little Presbyterian chapel built in 1728, a square brick building standing in a graveyard. The Fullers, local lords of the manor with strong Presbyterian sympathies, had provided a barn for services held by certain ejected ministers in the district. The numbers grew until by 1717 there was a congregation of about two hundred and in 1728 the present meeting house was built in the orchard of Joseph Fuller. This little chapel started the first school in the village in 1827. In 1865 the church was slightly altered, two porches being added and the pulpit moved from east to west, which necessitated the removal of one of the three galleries. An article by the Rev. R. D. Whitehorn in the *Journal of the Presbyterian Historical Society for 1929* gives much more information about this chapel.

In the Horsefair at **Bristol,** flanked by modern shops but set back from the street, is the first completely new Methodist building, the New Room. Built in 1739, the first intention was that it should simply be a society room but by 1748 space was so limited that the whole building was reconstructed and enlarged to what is now its present state: 'The interior has tall Tuscan columns, originally four, now six. The original four columns carry the octagonal lantern in the middle. Two galleries along the long sides. Pulpit arrangements at the north end with pretty staircase railings. The pale green colour was found by Sir George Oatley under later layers and accurately renewed' (Pevsner, *North Somerset and Bristol,* 1958). The top floor had provision for study, a dining room and bedrooms, all for the travelling preachers. The chapel is preserved in immaculate condition and visitors are made very welcome and many interesting Methodist relics are preserved. Maldwyn Edwards's booklet *New Room* (1972) gives much information about the history of the building.

The Unitarian chapel, built in 1717 in **Framlingham,** Suffolk, is but one of the many attractions of this delightful market town. Built of red and blue brick it is plain but elegant, with two storeys. The second floor has three widely spaced windows, while the ground floor has one window set between two doors, one of which has been bricked up. The small gallery is boxed in below to form a lobby. Balanced on a ball over the pulpit is a painted dove, well illustrated on the dust cover of Lindley's book and looking as he says 'like a fairground ornament'.

To the west of Sheffield in the village of **Stannington** is the Underbank Unitarian chapel. Built in 1742, this is a good example of a village chapel of the period and externally at least it has probably not been altered very much. The chapel, which is built of local stone, darkened by the atmosphere, lies below the level of the road. A graveyard with elm and beech trees surrounds the chapel. The chapel has a six-bay front with two doors; in the middle are two large round-headed windows, over the two doors are two small circular windows, while the two windows on the outside are two-storeyed. On the other side of the road is a village school built in 1853 and together the two buildings make a pleasant group, rather over-shadowed by the suburbs of Sheffield which are encroaching closely. The interior of this chapel appears to have been much restored and spoiled.

From a small village chapel we turn to the Octagon chapel, **Norwich,** the most elegant chapel of all, happily still standing and built in 1754-6 for Dr Taylor's wealthy and influential Unitarian congregation. Thomas Ivory, a builder and timber merchant, was the winner of the architectural competition and was in charge of the building, the cost of which was to be £5,000. (The rather unusual octagonal plan, though not uncommon in the early years of Christianity, had not been used for some centuries, though it is worth recalling that Wren's Great Model Plan of 1673 for rebuilding St Paul's was octagonal, though it was never built.) The exterior portico of the chapel is Greek Ionic. The eight internal columns, each a single tree trunk, are fluted Greek Corinthian; connected by round arches, they hold up the cupola. The roof is a unique construction: 'In the centre stands an upright king-post, into which are fitted eight horizontal beams, the end of each resting on the top of one of the eight pillars of the chapel. Radiating from the king-post are timbers slanting to other posts standing on the horizontal beams and from these posts other timbers slant to the roof. The king-post, which stands at the highest point of the domed ceiling, looks like a forest tree growing on the top of a little hill' (Drummond, *RIBA Journal,* vol 45, 1938).

In John Wesley's *Journal* for 23rd November 1757, we find the entry: 'I was shown Dr Taylor's new meeting house, perhaps the most elegant one in Europe. It is eight square, built of the finest brick, with sixteen sash windows below, as many above and eight skylights in the dome, which, indeed, are purely ornamental. The inside is finished in the highest taste and is as clean as any nobleman's saloon. The communion table is fine mahogany; the very latches on the pew doors are polished brass. How can it be thought that the old coarse Gospel should gain admission here.'

It seems clear that Wesley was impressed by the Octagon, all the more so when one notices that four years later he began what has been called the Era of the Octagon Chapels. Many chapels were built in the octagonal style but the majority have now gone. Two at least still remain; the **Yarm** Octagon in Cleveland, built in approximately 1763, and the **Heptonstall** Octagon in West Yorkshire, built at about the same time, are still in use. The Wesley octagons were built on a much slenderer budget than the Norwich octagon; the Nottingham octagon, for instance was built for £128 2s 7d. However, after about 1776, we find that the octagonal plan had gone out of fashion. Many reasons have been suggested for this. Methodism was becoming more sacramental and an octagonal shape made the organisation of a communion service more difficult. The building of octagonal chapels and more especially their roofs presented difficulty to the small builders usually entrusted with chapels. (At Heptonstall, the local builder was unable to make the roof, so it was made at Rotherham, carried across country and hauled up the hill by the villagers.) There were also practical limitations of size; by the 1780s, too, the Methodist movement was growing rapidly and chapels were being built capable of holding more than the old octagons. Octagon chapels were also difficult to enlarge.

In 1778 there was built in City Road, **London,** what has become known as Wesley's Chapel. Methodist teaching in London had previously been centred on the Foundery, a building on the boundary of Moorfields, which is no longer in existence. The builder of the chapel was Samuel Tooth, who was himself a Methodist local preacher, and the whole of the Methodist connexion responded to the appeal for subscriptions; the London Methodists alone subscribed £1,000. Wesley himself laid the foundation stone on 21st April 1777, in pouring rain, and on Sunday 1st November 1778 the chapel was opened. The standard edition of Wesley's *Journal* says (vol. 6, p 215-6): 'The chapel is perfectly neat but not fine and contains far more people than the Foundery. Many were afraid that the multitude, crowding from all parts, would have occasioned much disturbance. But they were happily disappointed; there was none at all. All was quietness, decency and order. I preached on part of Solomon's prayer at the dedication of the temple.'

A contemporary gloss on the proceedings is supplied by a newspaper report: 'The first quarter of an hour of his sermon was addressed to his numerous female auditory on the absurdity of the enormous dressing of their heads; and his religious labours have so much converted the women who attended at that place of worship that widows, wives and young ladies appeared on Sunday without curls, without flying caps and without feathers; and our correspondent further says that the female sex never made a more pleasing appearance.'

The chapel is 83 feet long by 58 feet wide and has the communion table in a semi-elliptical apse, enclosed by a balustraded rail. The three-sided gallery was, until the end of the eighteenth century, square, then the front of the west end of the gallery was made oval and the pews around the west end arranged in oval form. The gallery was supported by seven columns, given by George III, which had formerly been masts of warships; the columns were covered with plaster and painted to look like marble. The masts were superseded by marble columns and they now stand in the vestry, perhaps a little out of place. The pulpit, originally a three-decker and 15 feet tall, was reduced to 10 feet in 1864. The pulpit stands centrally in front of the communion table and the choir seats, font and lectern are in front of it. Prior to 1882 there was no organ and the singing was led by a precentor who used the lowest stage of the pulpit and had a tuning fork. Over the years, many changes have been made to the chapel, mostly by way of elaboration. The Greek Doric porch was added about 1809 and in 1864 many alterations were made: the old high-backed pews were replaced by low ones; and a space at the back which had been left as standing room for late comers was fitted with pews.

If we have dwelt at rather more length than usual on Wesley's Chapel, it is because it has, in the opinion of many, exercised much influence on Methodist architecture in particular and nonconformist architecture in general. It may be said to be typical of nonconformist architecture before the Gothic revival and it represents a step forward for the Methodists. Previous chapels had mainly been society rooms, whose mid-week activities had supplemented the Anglican services and not conflicted with them. By the time Wesley's

Chapel was built it was becoming apparent that the Methodists, who had never considered themselves dissenters, were not welcomed at communion by the average Anglican clergyman. So as the Methodists grew in numbers, its members felt increasingly unwelcome in the Church of England and it was with this feeling in mind that provision was made at Wesley's Chapel for the full Anglican order of service—though it was not until 1820 that an unordained minister, Jabez Bunting, was allowed to take a communion service there. The City Road pattern seems to have been followed for at least forty years after Wesley's death in 1797, probably as a result of a conference minute of 1790 which decided that all preaching houses in the future were to be built on the same plan as the London or Bath chapel.

Considering its position in Methodism and the influence it has had in the past, it is sad to relate that by 1972 the chapel was in such a bad state that it was condemned as unfit for public use. An appeal was launched to raise funds for the restoration and on November 1st 1978, exactly two hundred years since the original opening, the restored chapel was re-opened in the presence of HM The Queen and HRH The Duke of Edinburgh.

If we seem to have concerned ourselves overmuch with large city chapels at the expense of the smaller chapels which were being built in the countryside at this period, this is not because they were more important, but because they are better documented and it is easier to find out information about them.

The *Journal* of John Wesley for 5th July 1779 reads: 'In the afternoon we went to **Raithby.** It is a small village on top of a hill. The shell of Mr Brackenbury's house is finished, near which he has built a little chapel.' The 'little chapel' is still there, built over a stable, in a corner of the courtyard of Raithby Hall, built by Robert Carr Brackenbury (1752-1818). The chapel is 40 feet long by 18 feet wide and seats about ninety people. Six of the original pews still remain there, as does the pulpit sounding board and panelling. Brackenbury was a strange combination, a Lincolnshire squire, owner of many acres and friend of Wesley; he was also a keen local preacher who travelled many miles preaching in Wesley's service and who was largely responsible for the introduction of Methodism to the Channel Isles.

Melbourne, an attractive village south of Derby, has, in addition to the hall and gardens for which it is justly famous, a well-preserved Baptist chapel of 1750, enlarged in 1833. This is still in use, as is the Sunday school built in 1810. The chapel, which holds seven hundred people, is a plain gabled stone building with square-headed windows and is sombre but tasteful. Nonconformity seems to have been quite a factor in the social life of Melbourne, since the population, which in 1891 was 3,369, could boast besides the Baptist chapel, a Congregational chapel, a Wesleyan chapel, a New Jerusalem chapel built in 1863, and a Swedenborgian chapel. There was also a Baptist mission hall and fourteen memorial cottages built by Thomas Cook, of Cook's Tours fame. Melbourne's most famous son and a keen temperance worker, Cook made his entry into the field of organising excursions with tours organised to temperance rallies.

---

4. The nineteenth century and after

With the nineteenth century comes the age of chapel building. While the Church of England was gradually reviving, the numbers of Methodists were greatly increasing (from 80,000 in England and Wales in 1791 to 338,000 in 1848); it was an age of industrial expansion and population movement from the countryside to the new industrial towns which had in general been badly served by the Church of England in the past. The Methodists in particular were not slow to take advantage of this opportunity to bring the Gospel to the new town-dwellers, nor to take advantage of the deficiencies of Anglican church provision in the countryside (Cornwall is a good example here; many chapels were built by the Wesleyan Methodists and Bible Christians).

Belper, an expanding textile centre in Derbyshire, had a population of 7,235 in 1821 and no Anglican church until 1822. It supported no less than six kinds of dissenting church in the 1820s, a Unitarian, a Congregational, Wesleyan and Primitive Methodist and General and Particular Baptist. The Wesleyan chapel, built in 1807, is a good example of the small urban chapel. It is exactly 53 feet square and holds 630 people, many in the gallery which runs round three sides. Built of local stone, the chapel replaces the first Belper chapel, built on land given by Thomas Slater, a local Methodist farmer, in 1780. (Slater seems to have been one of the first Methodists in the area and opened his farm at nearby Shottle for use as a chapel in 1767. The farm, Chapel Farm, Shottle, is still there.) The chapel has been redecorated recently in very good taste and is one of the most attractive features of the town.

It has been said that 'Dissenting architecture is merely a reflection of the domestic architecture of the period, except when it imitates Anglican architecture, and then it is a generation too late' (quoted in Horton Davies, *Worship and Theology,* vol. 4). The Belper chapel fits in well with this generalisation as do many of the early chapels of the Primitive Methodists; their first chapel at Tunstall, Staffordshire, was built so that, if not wanted at a later date, it would easily convert to four houses. (Many pictures of these early 'domestic' chapels are to be seen in Kendall's *Origins and History of the Primitive Methodist Church* (two volumes), 1905. An early example of a Primitive Methodist chapel, built in 1832 and still standing in its original state, is the chapel at **Kniveton,** near Ashbourne, Derbyshire. Though even now but a small village, Kniveton was until 1860 the head of the circuit, until the building of a large chapel at Wirksworth resulted in a change. This small chapel, brick-built, with a hipped roof and round-headed twelve-lighted windows is still used and stands above the village.

The East Anglian countryside has many small country 'domestic-style' chapels and mention must be made of the Strict Baptist chapel at **Fressingfield,** near Halesworth in Suffolk. Built in 1835, the chapel has a most unusual coffin shape. A number of explanations have been given for its shape but the one most commonly held is that it would be an object lesson to the mortality of life. (The Strict Baptist chapel at **Friston,** also in Suffolk, is built to the same shape.) Despite the depressing nature of its shape, this humble red-brick chapel which stands in a graveyard is a most attractive feature in a delightful village. At nearby **Laxfield** is another Strict Baptist chapel built in 1807, a stylish domestic-looking chapel, with hipped roof, pantiles and two front entrances. At **Aldeburgh,** not far away, the Union Baptist chapel of 1822 has been described by E. M. Forster as 'a dignified and convenient building, very pleasant to speak in'. Standing near the beach and painted in chocolate and cream, the chapel is one of the many minor gems of this Suffolk coastal town.

We turn now to nonconformist imitations of Anglican architecture. After 1815 two parallel movements can be seen in church architecture, the Greek Revival and the Gothic Revival. The Greek Revival did not last long in Anglican architecture and examples are hard to find, the most famous being St Pancras parish church by H. W. and W. Inwood, built 1819-22. Greek Revival chapels were being built until well into the 1860s but some of the best examples have not survived—Carr's Lane Congregational Church, which was the first to be built, has been demolished. Of the Great Thornton Street Independent Chapel at Hull, built in 1841 by Lockwood and Allom and now demolished, the *Illustrated*

London News of the time said: 'The design presents a striking improvement on the general style and character of places of worship not belonging to the established church and shows the great advance of refinement and taste in the fine arts observable among dissenters.' (This chapel was a Corinthian temple with a frontage of 160 feet and had an auditorium holding 1800.)

A similar church which fortunately still survives was built in **Bristol** in 1839-40 by R. S. Pope and stands in Colston Avenue. Built for the Catholic and Apostolic Church, it is now a Roman Catholic church and called St Mary's on the Quay.

At the same time, 1839-40, the **York** Methodists built their Centenary Chapel in St Saviourgate. The architect was James Simpson of Leeds. The building is 90 feet by 68 feet and has an Ionic portico. The elegance of the facade is rather diminished by the fact that the sides are of brick. The interior is suitably magnificent, the organ and pulpit being in Spanish mahogany. The chapel is stirrup-shaped, the organ being on the straight (street) side. Nine pillars which support the gallery have gilt Corinthian capitals. There is an elaborate, partly coffered ceiling, set with acanthus-leaf bosses and a floral frieze in blue and white.

Another classical chapel—the details may be called 'debased Grecian', according to Pevsner—is the Particular Baptist chapel, now the Adult Education Centre, in Belvoir Street, **Leicester.** Built in 1845 by Joseph Aloysius Hansom, the Roman Catholic architect of Birmingham Town Hall and inventor of the hansom cab, it is certainly an original building and probably one of the few dissenting chapels built by a Catholic. The chapel, circular in shape, was locally known as the 'pork-pie chapel'. It is brick, stuccoed and has giant Tuscan columns. Its opening seems to have created quite an impact locally: 'The chapel opened on the 15th and the opening service began at seven a.m. at which a large congregation was present. At eleven when the congregation assembled again, the chapel was crowded in every part. Arrangements had been made with the Midland Railway for special trains from the stations on their line, the result of which was manifest in the large audience now assembled.' After a public dinner in the afternoon 'the chapel was again full for the evening service. When lit up with gas it presented a brilliant appearance. The total collections for the day were £760 and it is computed that over two thousand people were present for the principal service and many hundreds could not obtain entrance' (*Illustrated London News*, 1845).

In the 1850s, Sir Titus Salt, textile manufacturer and

Congregationalist, built a model village, **Saltaire,** near Bingley in West Yorkshire. The estate architects were Lockwood and Mawson of Leeds, who in 1858-9 built the Saltaire Congregational Church, a bizarre building, which according to Pevsner in *Yorkshire: West Riding* (1959) is the only aesthetically satisfying building in the village. It has, Pevsner continues, 'a grand semicircular portico and circular tower on a stumpy base. Domed family mausoleum on the North side. The interior is aisleless with giant Corinthian columns attached to the wall and a tunnel vault with penetrations.' (Lockwood and Mawson built the City Temple in London in 1874, still using this debased classical style.)

Let us now look at the Gothic Revival and its effect on chapel building. The Gothic Revival, which began as a literary rather than an architectural enthusiasm, when it spread to architecture first affected domestic buildings. Gentlemen 'gothicised' their mansions, as did Beckford with Fonthill, but the fashion only spread to Anglican churches when in 1818 an Act of Parliament authorised the expenditure of a million pounds for church building. Of the 214 'commissioners' churches' that were built, 174 were built in Gothic, partly because Gothic churches could be built more cheaply in brick than classical churches, which demanded more expensive stone for porticoes and pediments. While the Gothic Revival is often associated with the Ecclesiologists and the Anglo-Catholic wing of the Church of England, this did not come until later. One cannot otherwise imagine that Gothic would have become so popular in dissenting circles had it been associated exclusively with near-Romish tendencies. Perhaps, however, these arguments are academic and the main reason that Gothic chapels were built was cheapness and the desire to prove that dissenters could have churches as good as the Anglicans.

One of the earliest Gothic chapels was the Highbury Chapel, **Bristol,** built in 1842 and designed by William Butterfield. It was Butterfield's first and only dissenting commission and was probably gained for him through the influence of his uncle, W. D. Wills, the tobacco manufacturer and Congregationalist. It was built in the Perpendicular style and has a wide nave and aisles. (The polygonal apse and south tower were built in 1863 by Edward Godwin.) There is a monument designed by Eric Gill, showing a seated shepherd and three lambs under a canopy and dated 1924. The chapel which was damaged in the war was for some time redundant. It was fortunate that a suitable use was found for this important building, which has now been taken over by the Church of England.

A slightly earlier Gothic chapel in **Manchester** is the Upper Brook Street Chapel, built by Sir Charles Barry, architect of the new Houses of Parliament, for the Unitarians in 1839. It was however only outwardly Gothic, as the pulpit still stood in the middle of the end wall with the pews facing. The chapel now belongs to the Jehovah's Witnesses. The first nonconformist church to be internally and externally Gothic, and to have the altar in the chancel and the pulpit placed to one side, was the Unitarian Chapel in Stockport Road, **Gee Cross**, near Hyde, Greater Manchester. The same architects, Bowman and Crowther of Manchester, built Mill Hill Unitarian Chapel in City Square, **Leeds,** in 1847. This, too, has an altar in the chancel and was one of the first nonconformist chapels to use stained glass.

Some of the most interesting and dramatic Gothic churches built in the nineteenth century were built for the Catholic and Apostolic Church. W. McIntosh Brook built a church for them at **Albury,** Surrey, paid for by Henry Drummond, the local landlord and a firm supporter of the Irvingites.

The most magnificent church ever built for the Irvingites was opened on Christmas Eve 1853 in Gordon Square, **London.** It was designed by Raphael Brandon and intended to be the central building of the church: 'The church itself is a noble building in the Early English style, admirably adapted in its ample arrangements and its lofty proportions for dignified services conducted by a large staff of clergy and sustained with music' (*Irvingism* by E. Miller, 1878). It is indeed on a grand scale, being 212 feet long and 77 feet wide. The tower and spire were to rise to 300 feet but the spire was never built, presumably for lack of funds. The estimated cost of this church was £30,000 and it is now used by the Church of England.

One of the most forthright nonconformist sects has always been the Salvation Army but since the Army is only just over a hundred years old few of its buildings have any historic value and fewer still, it must be confessed, any architectural value. One of the most elaborate citadels was that built at **Aberdeen** in 1893-6. The architect was James Souttar. The style is said to be 'debased Balmoral baronial'. It was built of ashlar and is four-storeyed with an attic; the hall runs through three storeys. There is a five-storey tower, which is the chief architectural feature. 'On three corners, it is finished with small circular towers with ornamental finials but on the north-west corner there is a large turret rising a considerable height above the others and finished with an embattled course on the walls' (*Aberdeen Journal,* 20th June

1896). The ground floor was used for shop premises and the upper floors by the Salvationists. Another striking citadel is the one built at **Lincoln** in 1912. Its facade, which fronts on to one of the main streets, is castellated and of the five windows on the front all are different. The main window above the entrance is round-headed and is flanked by a round and an oblong window, while of the ground-floor windows, one is round-headed and the other square-headed.

Further along the same street is the slightly earlier chapel built by the Primitive Methodists in 1905 and still in use as the **Lincoln** Central Methodist Church. If the Kniveton chapel is Primitive Methodism at its most simple, this is Primitive Methodism at its most opulent. It was built as a replacement for the old chapel in Portland Place. The cost was £12,000. Its striking frontage and its cupola are landmarks in the High Street.

5. The Friends' meeting house

While in general it is difficult to distinguish between various styles of nonconformist architecture, the meeting houses built by the Quakers by their very lack of ostentation stand apart and it would seem sensible to describe them separately.

The Quakers have no liturgy or set services and all that was needed for a Quaker service was seating and a stand, or platform, for the elders to sit on. The seating was usually plain though on occasion the bench-ends were ornamented. As in chapels, the men and women sat on different sides of the meeting house; some have suggested that the women always sat furthest from the door in case of attacks, which in the early days were quite frequent. Joseph Besse's *Collection of the Sufferings* (1753) gives many such examples, of which the Derbyshire incident quoted below is typical. It occurred in 1659. 'Three days later there was a Meeting in the High-Peak to which came a Constable with Soldiers and plucked down Elizabeth Deane then praying, dragging her out of doors and shamefully tearing her clothes. With like Violence they drew out the rest some by the Hair of their Head, others by the Legs with their Heads on the Ground.' These people were imprisoned in Derby; in view of this persecution it is not surprising that the early meeting houses did not advertise themselves.

As far as can be told, the oldest building still in use as a meeting house is a Tudor farmhouse with the unquakerly name of the **Blue Idol.** It is situated near Coolham. With the exception of extensions at one end, it is in a good state of preservation and is said to be much the same as in Penn's day. It is said to have been a sixteenth-century farm of which one end was converted by John Shaw in 1691 for use as a meeting house. The stand is in one corner and is of an unusually uncomfortable design.

Another early meeting house was built in 1673 in **Cirencester** and despite alterations in 1726, 1810 and 1865, it retains much charm. The original meeting house was a small rectangular stone building and it is still in this room that meetings for worship are held. The Cotswold slated roof was steeply pitched but the later additions are pitched less steeply. There is a good account of the meeting house in *Cirencester Quakers, 1655-1973* (1973) by Leslie Stephen. Among the prominent members of the meeting was John Roberts (1623-83), who fought for Cromwell and was later converted to Quakerism. A new edition of the *Memoirs of the Life of John Roberts* has recently been published. These two books give a lively picture of the early Quakers.

The **Hertford** Meeting House was built in 1670 and is thus the oldest purpose-built meeting house which is still in use. It remains a mystery why it was decided to build during what must have been a period of persecution. Built in a very domestic style, the meeting house is of the same material as the surrounding houses. There are three-light mullioned windows and the loft is over the lobby with movable shutters so that the people could overflow into the loft or lobby as necessary. This is rather large for an early meeting house, but as four hundred Friends were said to be meeting in 1669 a large one was needed.

South-west of Sedbergh in Cumbria is the **Briggflatts** meeting house, one of the most famous of the early meeting houses. There is a date of 1675 on the porch. The loft is three-sided with open balusters, with steps up to it; by the side of the stairs are a unique feature, a pen for worshippers' dogs. Briggflatts was already a centre for 'Seekers' when George Fox paid his first visit there in 1653 and the numbers of Friends grew so fast that the meeting house was built. It is said that Fox preached in the meeting house in 1677 with six hundred present. The meeting house is substantially original, though minor renovations were made in 1905—the floor is no longer bare earth.

Perhaps the best known of all the Friends' meeting houses is the meeting house at **Jordans,** near Chalfont St Giles in Buckinghamshire. Built in 1688 it attracts many pilgrims, particularly from America, who come to see the grave of William Penn in the burial ground by the meeting house. The meeting house itself is a plain red-brick building with shutters at the windows, situated at the bottom of the valley and with trees at its sides. Its whitewashed interior and its benches of plain wood have a simple dignity. In the days before the meeting house was built Old Jordans Farm was used for Quaker meetings. In the Chalfont district lived several well known Quakers, including Thomas Ellwood, who was at one time Latin secretary to John Milton (who also lived at Chalfont St Giles for a time and whose cottage still stands there), Isaac Penington, son of a judge and author of devotional treatises, and of course William Penn, whose grave, together with those of his two wives, is in the burial ground.

A much less well-known meeting house is the **Brant Broughton** meeting house in Lincolnshire. The original barn was given to be used as a meeting house by Thomas Robinson in 1701 and the adjoining burial ground willed to the meeting house in 1727. The interior of the meeting house is painted white. The white seats are plain wood with backs. Besides the meeting room there are two smaller rooms, one used as a cloakroom, the other as a gallery. Outside there is stabling for a number of horses; (this is a common feature of remote country meeting houses and stables may be seen in Lancashire at Yealand Conyers and in Cumbria at Swarthmoor and Pardshaw). The original barn was built of brick and stone and was thatched but the thatch has been replaced by tiles.

One of the quaintest and best situated meeting houses is **Come to Good,** near Kea in Cornwall. 'There surrounded by sheltering trees stands the old meeting house. Its high thatched roof projects, like a bushy eyebrow, over the low white walls and thick white buttresses, shading the three narrow casement windows of pale green glass with their diamond lattice panes' (L. V. Hodgkin, *Book of Quaker Saints,* 1917). The English Place Name Society derive the name from Cwm ty Coit (the coomb by the dwelling in the wood). The meeting house was built in 1710 at a cost of £53 8s 3d and the gallery was added in 1717 at a cost of £15 10s 0d. The original meeting house was a plain rectangular building of about 20 feet by 27 feet, built of whitewashed rock and covered with thatch. The extensions at both ends were probably made at a later date. The entrance is at the west end of the church under the gallery with a timbered loft for protection. The loft, one of the most primitive types, is supported by two wooden posts and is reached by a steep staircase in the corner.

Another attractive thatched meeting house built in the same period 1710-16 is to be seen in the parish of Llandegley, in Powys. **The Pales** meeting house, as it is called, adds another attraction to this rather remote and little explored county.

Warwickshire has two of the best small meeting houses. At **Ettington,** near Stratford-upon-Avon, is the smallest meeting house in the country, built in 1681. It is a single room without lobby or loft and measures 23 feet by 16 feet. At nearby **Armscote** is another small meeting house, still used occasionally, which is said to be a conversion made in 1705 of a 1670 house.

Derbyshire has two interesting small meeting houses, now no longer used as such. **Monyash** meeting house, which is now a barn, was only a little larger than Ettington, and is complete with a loft and lobby. **Furness Toadhole,** near Wessington, and built in 1743, is one of the only two meeting houses known to have an external staircase to the loft. It now has a later dwelling house attached to it.

Generally speaking the most interesting examples of Quaker meeting houses date from the first hundred and fifty years of the society. The larger examples built later in the growing towns tended to lose something of the intimate simplicity associated with the early buildings. In the nineteenth century there were signs of a tendency to move towards a more conventional style of 'chapel' architecture but in general Friends avoided the worst excesses of the Gothic Revival (Thomas Rickman, the distinguished Gothic Revival architect, never built a Friends' meeting house, although he was a Quaker himself.)

For a final look at Friends' architecture let us consider the meeting house at **Bournville,** Birmingham, which is a long way from the mainstream of Quaker building—indeed it has been unkindly called the 'cathedral of Quakerism'. It was built in 1905 by W. Alexander Harvey, who was the consultant architect to George Cadbury and who had designed most of Bournville village, a village built by George Cadbury to provide for the employees of his chocolate factory. The meeting house was built in 'red-brick with stone dressings. The main hall is rectangular in plan but the subsidiary rooms are placed in short gabled wings obliquely on the angles of the main front, and an octagonal staircase turret with a high pointed tile cap stands in the north-west corner, resulting in an effective composition for its position at the highest point of the green. The west facade to the hall has a high gable with a two-light mullioned window divided by transoms, with below a round archway with several chamfers, tiny, two-light mullioned windows to either side. The side elevations to the hall have dormer windows and sloping buttresses. The interior is plain except for the most interesting roof trusses'

1. *The old Baptist chapel in Tewkesbury, Gloucestershire, is a late
seventeenth-century conversion of a medieval house.*

2. *The interior of the old Baptist chapel, Tewkesbury, has been faithfully restored.*

3. Bramhope chapel, West Yorkshire, was built as a Presbyterian chapel in 1649. Later it became Anglican.

4. The interior of Bramhope chapel, showing the box pews and the font.

5. The Congregational 'Old Meeting' in Colegate, Norwich, dates from 1693.

6. The Congregational chapel at Walpole, Suffolk, was converted from a house in the late seventeenth century.

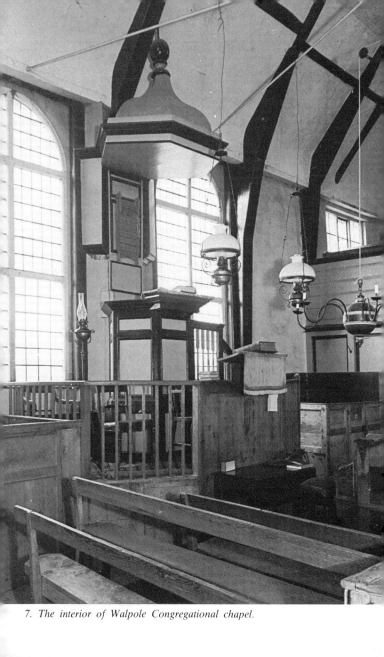

7. *The interior of Walpole Congregational chapel.*

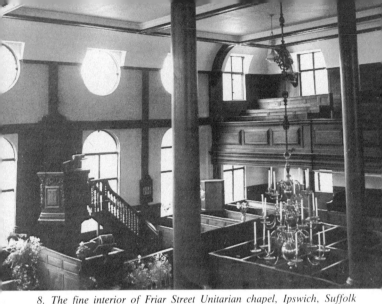

8. *The fine interior of Friar Street Unitarian chapel, Ipswich, Suffolk (1700).*

9. *The Baptist chapel of 1859 at Alcester, Warwickshire, was built next to the old chapel of 1636 (on the left).*

10. *An 1820 engraving of Wesley's chapel, City Road, Islington, London, opened in 1778 and restored in the 1970s.*

11. *The Pales Friends' Meeting House, Llandegley, Powys (1716).*

12. *The Unitarian chapel at Stannington, South Yorkshire, was built in 1742.*

13. *The oldest Methodist chapel is the New Room, Horsefair, Bristol, opened in 1778 and enlarged in 1748. It was restored in the 1970s.*

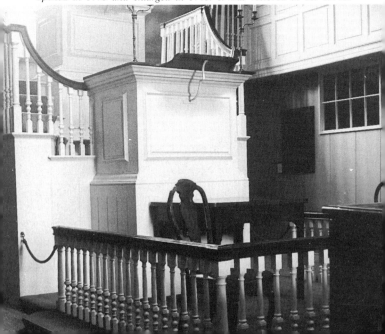

14. *The Particular Baptist chapel in Chenies, Buckinghamshire, opened in 1780.*

15. *Highbury Congregational chapel, Bristol, by William Butterfield (1842).*

16. *The United Reformed Church off Sheaf Street, Daventry, Northamp-tonshire, built as a Congregational chapel in 1722.*

17. *The United Reformed Church at Saltaire, West Yorkshire, was built in 1858-9 by Lockwood and Mawson as a Congregational chapel for Sir Titus Salt's model village.*

18. *Pithill Methodist chapel, built in 1854, was re-erected at Beamish, The North of England Open Air Museum, in 1990.*

19. *The Providence Methodist New Connexion chapel, Netherton, was built in 1837. In 1978 ii was re-erected in the Black Country Museum, Dudley, West Midlands.*

20. Capel Bethel (Welsh Baptist) in Baker Street, Aberystwyth, was opened in 1889.

21. *Briggflatts Friends' Meeting House, near Sedburgh, Cumbria (1675).*

22. *The Friends' Meeting House in Bournville, Birmingham, by W. A. Harvey (1905).*

23. *The Octagon Unitarian chapel, Norwich, built by Thomas Ivory in 1754-6, introduced a popular new style.*

24. *St Mary's on the Quay Roman Catholic Church, Colston Avenue, Bristol, was built 1839-40 in the Greek Revival style by R. S. Pope for the Catholic and Apostolic Church.*

25. *The octagonal Methodist chapel at Hepstonstall, West Yorkshire (1764). Chapels of this shape presented difficulties for local builders and the roof here had to be made many miles away in Rotherham.*

(*Warwickshire* by Sir N. Pevsner, 1967). The meeting house was lit from the start by electricity supplied from the factory. In 1915, in celebration of George Cadbury's silver wedding in 1913, an organ was installed, surely a unique possession for a Friends' meeting house. Following the death of George Cadbury in 1922, a niche was made in the south side of the meeting house to contain his ashes and a memorial bust. A little later, in 1924, a columbarium was made immediately behind the bust to contain the ashes of departed Friends. Opposite the columbarium is a garden of memory with a seat for meditation.

Seen in the light of Quaker building in the past this building may seem, externally at least, a little extravagant, but viewed in relation to the surrounding buildings we must agree that it fits in very well. If we see it as one small part of George Cadbury's ideal of 'ameliorating the condition of the working class, in and around Birmingham . . . by the provision of improved dwellings with gardens and open spaces to be enjoyed therewith' it can be regarded as a more than worthy part of the Quaker tradition.

6. Chapels in Wales

Though there are signs that its influence is waning, the chapel has become so much a part of the Welsh way of life as to become a cliche. Certainly a quick glance round any small Welsh town will reveal more nonconformist chapels than a comparable town in England. A single street in Holyhead, explored in the mid 1970s, yielded three chapels, two of which were practically opposite and built within five years of each other, the Tabernacle Newydd (Congregational) of 1865, its woodwork brightly painted in contrasting maroon and olive, and the English Baptist Chapel of 1861, a more subdued building altogether. A hundred yards further down was the English Presbyterian chapel of 1891, while a side street revealed a disused chapel of no apparent denomination but probably late nineteenth-century. If one considers that all these chapels are contained in one small area of a town whose present-day population is only eleven thousand it will show how large chapels loom in the Welsh landscape. If it be thought that the town or the area taken was untypical, it may be said that the number of chapels seen in the course of a journey taken recently from Bangor to Chester along the North Wales coast only confirmed the previous impression. As the scenery flashed by chapel succeeded chapel and every shade of the nonconformist spectrum seemed to be represented; grandiose chapels were followed by pebble-dashed village chapels and by shell-covered seaside chapels.

However, if we allow that Wales is filled with chapels, it may seem strange that there are not more pre-nineteenth-century ones and stranger still when we think that those that there are tend to be found in the counties of the Welsh border, e.g. Maes yr Onnen and the Pales in Powys. If we say that the reason is largely the result of the great success enjoyed by nonconformity in Wales, it may sound para-doxical, but it is to a great extent true. Original chapels in their pristine state usually only exist where chapel populations have never grown rapidly or become more prosperous. When the congregation becomes larger the usual result is the enlarge-ment of the original chapel or the building of a new one which quite often has not the architectural interest of the former. A sudden increase in prosperity could often result in the renovation of the interior and the abandoning of the old furniture and fittings.

Further difficulties lie in the path of the enquirer into the history of Welsh chapels. Pevsner's 'Buildings of England' series (Penguin, 1951 *et seq*), to which many references have been made in the course of this book, does not completely cover Wales. Only two volumes have appeared so far, *Powys* by Richard Haslam (1979) and *Clwyd* by the late Edward Hubbard (1986). A new volume may appear in 1992. Excellent for its area is *Thesis and Survey of the Nonconformist Chapel Architecture of Merthyr Tydfil* (1962) by Anthony Jones and he has since written *Welsh Chapels* (1984) under the auspices of the National Museum of Wales. This most attractively produced and illustrated book includes a list of Welsh chapels deserving preservation and, in many cases, the names of their architects. For the Welsh-speaking tourist *Capeli Cymru* by Penri Jones, published in the 'Welsh Travellers' series ('Cyfres Teithio Cymru') will be invaluable. John B. Hilling's *Historic Architec-ture of Wales* (1976) has a chapter on chapels, while more detail is provided by his *Architecture of the Welsh Chapel*, Transactions of the Honourable Society of Cymrodorion (1983). It is fortu-nate that the Shell Guides take an interest in chapel architecture but even here there are gaps as Glamorgan and Gwent have not so far been covered.

The Independent Church of **Llanvaches** in Gwent is generally regarded as the first nonconformist congregation in Wales. The chapel there was built in 1639 but the building there now does not seem to be original (according to Fellows's list 'only the eastern part seems to be original', while Dr Iorwerth Peate says 'completely modernised').

Another early chapel is near to Glasbury in Powys, the **Maes yr Onnen** Independent (Congregational) Chapel, built about 1696. The chapel is stone-built with a stone roof, and a cottage attached to it has a crook truss which can be seen in the chapel. This old chapel still contains its seventeenth-century furnishings. There are interesting associations here in that David Price who became minister at Maes yr Onnen in about 1700 maintained a school at Llwyn-llwyd in the parish of Llanigon nearby until he died in 1742. It was at this school that Howell Harris was educated between 1728 and 1730 and it is possible that some of his later evangelical fervour may have come from his education here. Here also was educated William Willams, Pantycelyn (author of the hymn 'Guide me, O thou great Jehovah' and the principal hymn-writer and poet of the Welsh Methodist Revival), probably between the years 1735 and 1738. The barn at which this nonconformist academy is thought to have been held is still to be seen at Llwyn-llwyd. Not very far from Llanigon is the parish of Talgarth and in this parish is **Trefecca,** where Howell Harris formed a religious settlement and built a chapel. Parts of the old buildings still remain and it is now a Methodist college. At College Farmhouse, formerly called Trevecka Isaf, the Countess of Huntingdon founded a college for followers of Howell Harris in 1768 and built a chapel. Across the mountains from Talgarth and not far (as the crow flies) is **Capel y Ffin**, where there is a small nonconformist meeting house, possibly the meeting house built by the persecuted Baptists in 1762.

Turning now from the border to Gwynedd, we find **Capel Newydd** in the parish of Llangian. This old chapel was built in 1769 and was the oldest Congregational chapel in the former county of Caernarvonshire. The chapel has the honest simplicity and lack of pretension that we have come to expect. There is a legend that the money for this chapel was provided by Catherine Edwards, the English widow of Timothy Edwards, a member of a local puritan family, but although this cannot be proved it is at least certain that she gave to Capel Newydd a gold communion cup which still exists and that she bought the land for an Independent chapel in Caernarvon. In the nineteenth century depopulation in the Capel Newydd district and in 1872 the building of the Independent chapel at Horeb, Mynytho, made it difficult for the old chapel to keep going and by the end of the nineteenth century it was used only occasionally. By 1952 the upkeep of the building was too much for the Mynytho Congregationalists and funds were raised for its restoration with the help of the Ministry of Works. It was reopened after the restoration in 1958 and is now used for cultural meetings, not necessarily religious activities. It still retains its earth floor and box pews and is rather difficult to find.

Also in Gwynedd, at **Tremadoc** is the Peniel Chapel of 1811; its bold Tuscan portico is quite a landmark. Built, as was most of the town, by William Madocks, MP for Boston, this rather lavish provision for dissenters caused some surprise to the Bishop of Bangor, as the Shell Guide tells us. Madocks assured the Bishop that the chapel was built on sand while the Anglican church, built in 1806, was built on rock (both are still standing). The raked interior is an unusual feature of this attractive chapel.

A less well-known chapel, near the junction of the B4589 and A475 at **Rhydowen** in Dyfed is the 1834 Unitarian chapel with round-headed double doors and sash windows; into the facade are built slate gravestones. This chapel is typical of many early nineteenth-century Welsh chapels. Sadly it is now closed and neglected.

About a mile from **Llanbedr,** in Gwynedd, is the Salem Baptist chapel, little known by name but well-known to many of the older generation at least through the painting *Salem* by S. C. Vosper, which was shown at the Royal Academy in 1909. Reproductions of the painting, which depicts a rather stern-looking lady in traditional Welsh dress holding a prayer-book, were very popular in many Welsh homes. The interior of this chapel and its congregation provided the setting and models for the picture and it is well worth a visit for its eighteenth-century air.

An unusual, not to say rare, chapel is the Beulah Chapel at **Margam,** West Glamorgan, which was built in 1838 on land given by Mr Talbot of Margam Hall on condition that the chapel should be built to his design. The chapel is octagonal and was built by one Thomas Jenkins for £100.

Another chapel of character is the 1820 Congregational chapel at **Ruthin,** Clwyd, whose bow-fronted facade lends a further attraction to this delightful little town. In **Carmarthen** the 1872 English Baptist Chapel in Lammas Street by George Morgan is very stylish. Set back from the street, its classical columns are more sophisticated than the usual Welsh chapel. Not as stylish, but attractive in its own way with its tower, is the English Presbyterian chapel at **Menai Bridge,** Gwynedd, which was opened in 1888 and was one of the first chapels in the island of Anglesey to possess a pipe organ.

Postscript to the second edition

Since 1975 there has been an awakening of interest in nonconformity and its architecture and chapels now receive the attention they deserve. In 1986 the first volume of Christopher Stell's *Inventory* (HMSO), covering central England, was published. Volume 2, which will cover south-west England, is in the press and volume 3, which will cover the north of England, is in preparation.

In London in September 1988 the Chapels Society was formed. The word chapel is used in its widest sense and covers Roman Catholic and Jewish buildings. Information can be obtained from the Secretary, Christopher Stell, Frognal, 25 Berks Hill, Chorleywood, Hertfordshire WD3 5AG.

In Wales in May 1986 Cymdeithas Treftadaeth Capeli (The Chapels Heritage Society), short title Capel, was formed. The Secretary is Dr D. Huw Owen of the National Library of Wales, Aberystwyth, Dyfed SY23 3BU. While Welsh is used at meetings at times, English translations are always provided and non-Welsh speakers are most welcome. Like its English counterpart it has two meetings a year and appears to be thriving. Both societies are not merely antiquarian but are interested in practical conservation.

Further reading

Arnold, H. G. 'Early Meeting Houses', *Transactions of the Ancient Monuments Society* , 1960.

Beazley, E., and Brett, L. *The Shell Guide to North Wales.* Faber, 1971.

Betjeman, J. *First and Last Loves.* Murray, 1952.

Binney, M., and Burman, P. *Chapels and Churches: Who Cares?* British Travel Association and Country Life, 1977.

Binney, M., and Burman, P. *Change and Decay: The Future of our Churches.* Studio Vista, 1977.

Briggs, M. *Puritan Architecture and its Future.* Lutterworth, 1946.

Butler, D. *Quaker Meeting Houses of the Lake Counties.* Friends' Historical Society, 1978.

Clack, P. A. G., and Pattinson, K. E. *Weardale Chapels.* Durham University Department of Archaeology, 1978.

Cox, B. *Chapels and Meeting Houses in the Vale of Evesham.* Vale of Evesham Historical Society, 1982.

Clegg, Reverend Dr J. *Diary, 1708-1755* (edited by V. Doe) . Three volumes. Derbyshire Record Society, 1978-81.

FURTHER READING

Davies, H. *Worship and Theology in England,* volumes 3 and 4. Oxford University Press, 1961-2.

Davies, E. T. *Religion and Society in the 19th Century* (New History of Wales series). C. Davies, 1981.

Dolbey, G. *Architectural Expression of Methodism.* Epworth, 1964.

Drummond, A. L. 'Century of Chapel Architecture', *Congregational Quarterly,* 1942.

Drummond, A. L. *The Church Architecture of Protestantism.* Clark, 1934.

Drummond, A. L. 'The English Meeting House', *RIBA Journal,* 1938.

Forty-second Interim Report. Royal Commission on Historic Monuments, 1985. A list of chapels and meeting houses deemed most worth preserving.

Hague, G. and J. *The Unitarian Heritage: an Architectural Survey.* Godfrey, 1986.

Hallelujah: Recording Chapels and Meeting Houses. Council for British Archaeology, 1985.

Haslam, R. *Powys* (The Buildings of Wales series). Penguin, 1979.

Hilling, J. B. *The Historic Architecture of Wales.* University of Wales, 1976.

Hilling, J. B. 'The Architecture of the Welsh Chapel', *Transactions of the Honourable Society of Cymrodorion,* 1983.

Hubbard, E. *Clwyd* (The Buildings of Wales series). Penguin, 1986.

Jones, A. *Welsh Chapels.* National Museum of Wales, 1984.

Jones, P. *Capeli Cymru* (Cyfres Teithio Cymru). Y Lolfa, 1980.

Lidbetter, H. *The Friends' Meeting House.* Sessions, second edition 1979.

Lindley, K. *Chapels and Meeting Houses.* Baker, 1969.

Nonconformist Chapels in Staffordshire. Staffordshire County Council, 1987.

Pevsner, N. Buildings of England series. Penguin, 1951-74.

Rees, V. *The Shell Guide to Mid-west Wales.* Faber, 1971.

Rees, V. *The Shell Guide to South-west Wales.* Faber, 1963.

Short, H. L. 'Changing Styles in Nonconformist Architecture', *The Listener,* 17th March 1955.

Steel, D. J. *Sources for Nonconformist Genealogy and Family History.* Society of Genealogists, 1973.

Stell, C. *An Inventory of Nonconformist Chapels and Meeting Houses in Central England.* Royal Commission on Historic Monuments. HMSO, 1986.

Stell, C. *Architects of Dissent: Some Nonconformist Patrons and Their Architects.* Dr Williams's Trust, 1976.

Verey, D. *The Shell Guide to Mid-Wales.* Penguin, 1960.

Gazetteer

Since the first publication of this book in 1975, the Royal Commission on Historic Monuments have published their Forty-second Interim Report (1985) which contains a list of chapels, arranged by county, which they considered to be most worthy of preservation. This list gives map references, dates and denominations and is the one to which the serious student should refer. It should be obtainable through local libraries. The list following is a personal selection and gives a sample of the many interesting buildings.

Abbreviations: B, Baptist; C, Congregational; CAC, Catholic and Apostolic Church; CE, Church of England; ch, chapel; CHC, Countess of Huntingdon's Connexion; CM, Calvinistic Methodist; FMH, Friends' meeting house; H, Huntingdonian; I, Independent; M, Methodist; MH, meeting house; Mvn, Moravian; NCGB, New Connexion of General Baptists; P, Presbyterian; PB, Particular Baptist; PlB, Plymouth Brethren; PM, Primitive Methodist; RC, Roman Catholic; SA, Salvation Army; SB, Strict Baptist; S & PB, Strict and Particular Baptist; U, Unitarian; URC, United Reformed Church; WM, Wesleyan Methodist; WR, Wesleyan Reform.

ENGLAND

AVON
Bath: the Vineyards, former CHC, 1765. Bristol: Broadmead, New Room, M 1739-48; Lewin's Mead, U 1787-91; Highbury ch, C 1842 by W. Butterfield; St Mary's on the Quay, CAC by R. S. Pope, now RC. Hambrook: C 1816.

BEDFORDSHIRE
Ampthill: former FMH, 1753. Bedford: Bunyan MH, rebuilt 1849-50. Cardington: M 1823. Carlton: SB 1760. Clifton: SB 1853. Pertenhall: Wood End, former Mvn 1827. Roxton: C, early 19th century, barn converted to chapel. Southill: SB 1805. Stevington: B 1720.

BERKSHIRE
Newbury: Northbrook Street, M 1837. Reading: St Mary's ch, former I 1798. Woodley and Sandford: Loddonbridge Road, URC 1834.

BUCKINGHAMSHIRE
Amersham: Whielden Street, FMH, early 17th century. Chalfont St Giles: Jordans, FMH 1688. Chenies: PB 1778. Haddenham: B 1810. Sherington: URC 1822. Winslow: Keech's MH, SB c.1695.

CAMBRIDGESHIRE
Bassingbourn: URC c.1791. Cambridge: Trumpington Street, Emmanuel, URC 1875 by James Cubitt. Ely: Chapel Street, CHC, early 19th century. Great Gransden: SB 1734. Melbourn: URC c.1717.

CHESHIRE
Great Warford: B, timber-framed barn converted 1712. Knutsford:

GAZETTEER

Brook Street, U 1689. Macclesfield: King Edward Street, U c.1689. Wilmslow: Dean Row, U 1693.

CLEVELAND
Stockton on Tees: Dovecot Street, FMH 1816. Yarm: M 1763 (octagon).

CORNWALL
Camborne-Redruth: Gwennap preaching pit, early 18th century. Kea: Come to Good, FMH c.1710. Marazion, FMH 1688. Penzance: Chapel Street, WM 1814. St Just: Chapel Road, WM 1833. Truro: Union Place, St Mary's, WM 1830.

CUMBRIA
Alston with Garrigill: Garrigill, 'Redwing chapel', C 1756, disused. Burgh by Sands: Moorhouse, former FMH 1733, now farm store. Carlisle: Lowther Street, c.1843. Claife: Colthouse, FMH c.1688. Cockermouth: URC 1850. Dean: Pardshaw, FMH 1729. Kendal: FMH 1816. Mungrisdale: Mosedale, FMH 1702. Ravenstonedale: URC, early 18th century. Sedbergh: Briggflatts, FMH 1675. Stainton: URC 1696. Ulverston: Swarthmoor, FMH 1688.

DERBYSHIRE
Belper: M 1807; Field Row U ch, 1788. Bonsall: B 1824. Charlesworth: C 1797. Chesterfield: Elder Yard, U 1694 (altered). Chinley: C 1711. Duffield: NCGB 1830. Melbourne: NCGB 1750, altered 1833. Monyash: former FMH 1773. Ockbrook: Mvn ch and settlement, 1752. Sawley: NCGB 1830 (nearby cottage with plaque, birthplace of Dr Clifford).

DEVON
Barnstaple: Bear Street, BC 1876; Grosvenor Street, PlB c.1840. Chulmleigh: C, early 18th century. Culmstock: Spiceland, FMH 1815. Dalwood: Loughwood, B c.1700 (National Trust, open). Exeter: South Street, George's MH, former U 1719 (shop); Sidwell Street, WM 1905. Exmouth: Point in View, C 1811. Plymouth: Mutley Plain, B 1869. Shebbear: lake, complex of chapel, graveyard, school, Bible Christian from 1815. Sidmouth: All Saints Road, U 1710. Torquay: Babbacombe Road, Wesley, former WM 1874; Torwood Gardens, former P 1863.

DORSET
Bridport: East Street, U 1794; South Street, FMH, early 18th century. Charmouth: C 1815. Lyme Regis: former C 1755 (exhibition). Sherborne: Long Street, former C 1804. Wareham: Church Street, C 1762.

DURHAM
Beamish, The North of England Open Air Museum: WM 1854 (re-erected here 1990). Darlington: Bondgate, M 1812; Skinnergate, FMH 1840. Hamsterley: B 1774.

EAST SUSSEX
Brighton: New Road, U 1830; Elim Tabernacle, 1820. Ditchling:

former U *c*.1740. Hastings: Ebenezer, PB 1817. Heathfield: Chapel Cross, H 1809. Lewes: Jireh Temple, H 1809.

ESSEX
Chelmsford: FMH 1826. Chipping Ongar: C 1833. Colchester: East Stockwell Street, former C 1817. Great Bardfield: FMH 1804. Harlow: B 1756. Little Baddow: URC 1707. Maldon: FMH 1821. Saffron Walden: former B 1792. Waltham Holy Cross: B 1836. Witham: B 1828; C 1840.

GLOUCESTERSHIRE
Blockley: B 1835. Cheltenham: Bethel, B 1820 (now Christadelphian); Salem, B 1843-4; Cambray, B 1853-5; Bayshill, U 1842-4 (now auction sale rooms). Cirencester: FMH 1673. Nailsworth: FMH 1689. Painswick: FMH 1705. Tewkesbury: B, late 17th-century conversion of medieval house; Barton Street, B 1805.

GREATER LONDON
City Road: Wesley's ch, M 1777. Gordon Square: CAC 1851-4 (now C E). Hampstead Garden Suburb: Free Church B and URC 1911, by Sir Edwin Lutyens. Newington Green: U 1708, altered 1860 (oldest remaining London MH). Upper Street: Union ch, C 1876, by James Cubitt.

GREATER MANCHESTER
Dimple (near Turton): U 1713. Dukinfield: U 1840-1. Fairfield (near Droylsden): Mvn settlement begun 1783. Hale: U 1723. Hyde: Gee Cross, U 1846, by Bowman and Crowther. Manchester: Victoria Park, former Christian Science 1903, by Edgar Wood; Upper Brook Street, former U 1837-9, by Sir Charles Barry (now Jehovah's Witnesses).

HAMPSHIRE
Alton: FMH *c*.1672. Hartley Wintney: B 1807-8. Mortimer West End: CHC 1798. Ringwood: former U 1727. Tadley: URC 1718, enlarged. Winchester: URC 1853.

HEREFORD AND WORCESTER
Almeley Wootton: FMH 1672. Bewdley: former P *c*.1778 (now RC Church of the Holy Family). Bromyard: URC 1701. Evesham: U 1737. Hereford: FMH 1822. Leominster: B 1771. Ross-on-Wye: FMH 1804. Worcester: former CHC 1804, enlarged 1815; former URC 1858.

HERTFORDSHIRE
Berkhamsted: FMH 1818. Hemel Hempstead: FMH, late 18th century. Hertford: FMH 1670 (oldest surviving FMH). Hitchin: Tilehurst Street, B 1844. St Albans: Spicer Street, C 1811.

HUMBERSIDE
Barrow upon Humber: Lord's Lane, former C *c*.1780 (now SA). Cottingham: C 1819. Epworth: Old Rectory (birthplace of John and Charles Wesley), 1710, with additions, restored 1956 and Wesley Memorial ch 1888-91. Hedon: B 1801.

GAZETTEER

ISLE OF WIGHT
Godshill: WM 1838. Newport: U 1774.

KENT
Chevening: Bessels Green, U 1716. Cranbrook: Providence ch, SB 1803-28. Dartford: Priory Hill, SB 1794. Dover: Adrian Street, U 1819. Tenterden: U 1746.

LANCASHIRE
Chorley: U 1725. Crawshaw Booth: FMH 1736. Goodshaw: former B, late 18th century (English Heritage). Lancaster: FMH 1708. Rivington: U 1703. Tunley: former P 1691 (now URC).

LEICESTERSHIRE
Hinckley: Great Meeting, U 1722. Husbands Bosworth: B 1807. Long Whatton: Diseworth B ch 1752 (early NCGB). Leicester: Belvoir Street, former PB 1845, by J. A. Hansom (now adult education centre). Market Harborough: URC 1844. Oakham: Gaol Street, FMH 1719.

LINCOLNSHIRE
Boston: Spain Lane, U 1819-20. Brant Broughton: FMH 1701; WR 1862. Gainsborough: FMH 1704-5, altered 1876; PM 1877, now SA. Lincoln: FMH 1689, altered in 18th century; Mint Street, B 1870; Newland, URC 1876; PM 1905; U 1725.

MERSEYSIDE
Liverpool: Gateacre, U 1700; Toxteth, U 1618, partly rebuilt 1774. Port Sunlight: Christ Church URC 1902-4, by W. and S. Owen for W. H. Lever. Thornton Hough: URC 1906 by J. Lomax-Simpson for W. H. Lever.

NORFOLK
Diss: FMH 1749; former U 1821 (now Masonic Hall). Holt: High Street, M 1862, by Thomas Jekyll. Little Walsingham: M 1793-4. North Walsham: Swafield FMH 1772. Norwich: Old Meeting, C 1693; Upper Goat Lane, FMH 1826; Octagon, U 1756 by Thomas Ivory. Thetford: C 1817. Wells-next-the-Sea: C 1816.

NORTHAMPTONSHIRE
Brigstock: School Lane, C 1798. Culworth: former Mvn 1809, now entirely transformed. Daventry: Sheaf Street, C 1722, now URC, altered. Middleton Cheney: B 1806. Milton Malsor: B 1827. Northampton: C 1695, altered 1862 and 1890 (Philip Doddridge's chapel). Thrapston: B 1787, enlarged in 19th century and interior altered. Walgrave: B 1788. Wellingborough: URC 1875, unique ovoid plan; FMH 1819.

NORTHUMBERLAND
Belford: P 1776. Berwick-upon-Tweed: P, early 19th century. Branton: P 1781. Coanwood: FMH 1760. Embleton: P 1833. Falstone: P 1807, rebuilt 1876. Norham: former P 1753 (now URC).

NORTH YORKSHIRE
Malton: B 1823; C 1815; FMH 1823. Osmotherley: M 1754. Scarborough: former FMH 1801. York: St Saviourgate, Centenary 1839, by James Simpson of Leeds; U 1693.

NOTTINGHAMSHIRE
Kirkby in Ashfield: B 1754, altered (early NCGB). Mansfield: Stockwell Gate, former M 1791 (now B); U 1701, altered; Quaker Lane, FMH rebuilt 1800. Nottingham: High Pavement, U 1874-6, by Stuart Colman (now lace museum). Southwell: Nottingham Road, B 1839. Tuxford: WM 1841. Wellow: PM 1847.

OXFORDSHIRE
Abingdon: B 1841; C 1862 (remains of *c.*1700 MH at rear). Aston Tirrold: URC, former P 1728. Banbury: FMH 1751. Barford St Michael: M 1840. Bicester: C 1729. Burford: B 1804; FMH 1709; M, baroque mansion converted to ch 1849. Chinnor: C 1805. Grove: SB *c.*1830. Hook Norton: B 1787. Oxford: B 1798; SA 1888. Sibford Gower: FMH 1678-81. Wallingford: C 1799. West Adderbury: FMH 1675.

SHROPSHIRE
Bridgnorth: B 1842. Broseley: Old Chapel, PB 1742. Ludlow: former C 1830 (now dwelling house). Madeley: M 1841. Newport: C 1817. Shrewsbury: U, late 17th century, rebuilt early 18th century, altered. Wem: C 1834. Weston Rhyn: URC 1858.

SOMERSET
Bridgwater: Dampiet Street, U 1788. Frome: Rook Lane, former C 1707; South Parade, B 1850. Ilminster: East Street, former U 1719. Long Sutton: FMH 1717. Street: FMH 1850. Taunton: Middle Street, Octagon, former WM 1776; Mary Street, U 1721. Watchet: B 1824.

SOUTH YORKSHIRE
Great Houghton: former P *c.*1650 now CE. Loxley: URC 1787. Sheffield: Upper ch, U 1700; Carver Street, M 1804. Stannington (near Sheffield): U 1742.

STAFFORDSHIRE
Armitage: URC 1820 (built for a private benefactor). Leek: Derby Street, C 1862-3, built by William Sugden; Overton Bank, FMH 1697. Newcastle under Lyme: U 1717. Oakamoor: Bolton Memorial ch, C 1878. Rushton: Cloud PM 1815 (one of the earliest PM chapels). Stafford: Foregate Street, FMH 1730. Tamworth: Victoria Road, U 1724.

SUFFOLK
Aldeburgh: Union B 1822. Bury St Edmunds: FMH 1750; U 1711-12 (now Pentecostal). Framlingham: U 1717. Fressingfield: SB 1835. Halesworth: Quay Street, URC 1836, by James Fenton. Ipswich: FMH 1700; U 1700. Laxfield: B 1807. Walpole: C (late 17th-century conversion with noteworthy interior). Woodbridge: C 1805; former FMH 1678 (now store room).

GAZETTEER

SURREY
Albury: The Apostles' ch, CAC 1840. Ash: C 1825. Charlwood: Providence ch, 1816. Dorking: West Street, C 1834. Esher: FMH 1797.

TYNE AND WEAR
Newcastle upon Tyne: Brunswick Place, M 1820-1; FMH, rebuilt 1805.

WARWICKSHIRE
Alcester: B 1736 (now hall), new ch 1859. Armscote: former FMH 1705. Atherstone: C 1827. Baddesley Ensor: former FMH 1722. Bedworth: Old MH, URC 1726-7. Ettington: FMH 1684. Leamington Spa: C 1836; B 1833. Polesworth: C 1828. Shipston on Stour: former FMH 1690 (now public library). Tanworth: Umberslade, Christ church, B 1877. Warwick: C 1798; FMH 1695; U 1781.

WEST MIDLANDS
Bournville: FMH 1905, by W. A. Harvey. Dudley: Black Country Museum, Netherton Providence New Connexion M, 1837 (re-erected here 1978). Stourbridge: U 1788; FMH 1698.

WEST SUSSEX
Billingshurst: U 1754. East Grinstead: Zion ch, CHC 1810. Horsham: FMH 1786; U 1721. Thakeham: Blue Idol FMH (1691 conversion of part of 16th-century house).

WEST YORKSHIRE
Ackworth: FMH 1847. Bramhope: former P 1649, later CE. Fulneck: Mvn 1748. Heckmondwike: Upper I ch, URC 1890. Heptonstall: M 1764 (octagon). Leeds: Mill Hill, U 1847, by Bowman and Crowther. Saltaire: URC 1858-9, by Lockwood and Mawson. Todmorden: U 1869, by John Gibson.

WILTSHIRE
Avebury: URC c.1707. Bradenstoke cum Clack: Providence ch, SB 1777. Bratton: B 1834, enlarged. Calne Without: Derry Hill 'Little Zoar', SB 1814. Corsham: Monks ch, URC, late 17th-century FMH converted 18th century (original interior). East Tytherton: Mvn 1792. Horningsham: C 18th century, thatched. Melksham: FMH 1734.

WALES

CLWYD
Bettisfield: PM 1870. Llandyrnog: Capel y Dyffryn, M 1836; B 1836. Mold: Pentref Welsh M 1828; Bethesda Welsh P 1863; URC 1863. Ruthin: Pendref C 1827, additions in 1875; Y Tabernacl Welsh P 1889-91. St Asaph: Ebenezer Welsh P 1843.

DYFED
Aberaeron: Tabernacle CM 1833-7. Aberystwyth: Baker Street, Capel Bethel Welsh B 1888-9; Baker Street, Seion C; Bath Street, St David's URC 1872; Queen's Road, Seilo P 1859-63 (new facade 1956). Cardigan: William Street, Bethania B 1847. Carmarthen: Lammas

Street, B 1872. Cilcennin: C 1859. Cilgerran: Penuel B 1862. Clydai: C 19th century (slate built). Fishguard: Hermon B 1776, restored 1832. Haverfordwest: Bethesda B 1878; Tabernacle C 1774. Llandewi Velfrey: B 1832. Llandissilio East: Rhydwilym B 1761. Llandovery: High Street, M 1886 (memorial ch to William Williams of Pantycelyn). Llanelli: Tabernacle C 1872. Llanfihangel a'r Arth: Tabernacle 1650, restored 1909. Llangeitho: Daniel Rowlands Memorial ch, 18th century. Llansadwrn: Libanus B 1841 (NW of village at Waun Clynda). New Quay: Towyn C 1860. Tregaron: (8 miles SE) Soar-y-Mynydd CM 1822. Tre'r-ddol: Yr Hen Gapel M 1844 (now a museum).

GLAMORGAN
Aberdare: Old MH 1751, rebuilt U 1862. Bridgend: Park Street, Old MH U 1795. Cardiff: The Hayes, Tabernacle B 1865; St Fagan's Museum, Dre-fach Felindre ch, Carmarthen, re-erected in museum. Clydach: Calfaria B 1868. Pontypridd: Tabernacle B 1861 (now heritage centre). Swansea: Morriston, Tabernacle C 1873; Mount Pleasant, B 1875. Ton Pentre: Bethesda C 1907.

GWENT
Beaufort: Capel Bethesda B 1828. Llanvaches: C 1639, rebuilt 1924. Mynyddislwyn: Siloh P 1813. Nantyglo: Bethel M 1827 (restored). Newbridge: Beulah 1809. Pontypool: Crane Street, B 1846.

GWYNEDD
Aberdaron: Capel Carmel B c.1818. Abererch: Ebenezer ch. Amlwch: English M. Bala: English P 18th century; Welsh P late 19th century (with statue of Thomas Charles [1755-1814] one of the founders of the British and Foreign Bible Society). Bangor: Capel Horeb 1826; B 1812. Bethesda: Siloam 1872; St Anne's 1865. Bryn-Siencyn: CM 1883. Caernarfon: Capel Moriah M 1826; B 1812. Criccieth: Capel Uchaf B 1791. Lechylched: Salem 1824, enlarged 1839 and 1900. Llanarmon: Capel Pencoed CM 1820. Llanbedr: Salem B 1850. Llandudno: Ebenezer M 1909. Llanerchymedd: Welsh P church of Jerusalem. Nanhoron, Llyn: Capel Newydd C c.1770. Tremadog: Peniel 1811.

POWYS
Brecon: Plough Independent 1841. Crickhowell: Bethabara B 1840. Cwmbelan: Zion 1827 (enlarged). Evenjobb: B 1849. Glasbury: Maes yr Onnen C 1696. Llandegley: The Pales FMH 1717. Llandrindod Wells: Caetach U 1715. Llanfyllin: Pendref C 1714, altered 1829. Llanidloes: Sion United Reformed church 1878; B 1876. Llanigon: Llwyn-llwyd barn, nonconformist school. Meifod: FMH 1701, restored. Newtown: B 1881. Pentrellifor: M 1798. Talgarth (6 miles SE): Capel y Ffin: B 1762. Trefecca: C M College.

Acknowledgements

There is not space here to list all the people who have been so helpful in providing information for this book but mention must be made of Mr Christopher Stell OBE, MA, B Arch, FRIBA, FSA. Mr Stell, author of the definitive work on the subject, checked my gazetteer of the English counties for the first edition of this book. He has been a constant source of advice and information ever since, as has Dr Clyde Binfield of Sheffield University, who supervised my thesis and has helped me in many ways over the past twenty years.

For this second edition I have had the help of Mr R. F. S. Thorne JP, C Eng, MICE, FSA of Ottery St Mary, Devon, and the benefit of his detailed and extensive knowledge of West Country nonconformity. He has re-checked and revised the gazetteer of Cornwall, Devon, Dorset and Somerset. For the section on Wales, I have had the expert advice of Mr John B. Hilling ARIBA, of Cardiff, who has corrected errors and suggested deficiencies. Any errors that remain in this book are my responsibility alone.

I should also like to thank my friends Mr Peter Gallimore, for providing me with some excellent photographs of remote chapels, and Mr Philip Burton BA, FLA. His knowledge of Dissent, his skill in proof reading, his topographical expertise and his prowess as a chauffeur have all been invaluable.

Finally most thanks of all must go to my wife Gwyneth for her forbearance and encouragement over the past years.

Photographs are acknowledged as follows: Peter Gallimore, plate 11; Jim Lawson of the Photographic Archive of Beamish: The North of England Open Air Museum, plate 9; Cadbury Lamb, cover and plates 1, 2, 14, 16, 17, 18, 19; Lidbetter Collection, Friends' House Library, plate 22; Norwich Public Library, plates 5, 23; John Ray, plate 10; *The Times*, plate 24. All other photographs are by the author.

Index

The following abbreviations are used in this Index: B, Baptist; C, Congregational; CAC, Catholic and Apostolic Church; FMH, Friends' meeting house; M, Methodist; P, Presbyterian; PB, Particular Baptist; PM, Primitive Methodist; SA, Salvation Army; SB, Strict Baptist; U, Unitarian; URC, United Reformed Church; WB, Welsh Baptist; WM, Wesleyan Methodist.

63